D0982791

The Soul's Sincere Desire

The Soul's Sincere Desire

The Soul's Sincere Desire

BY

GLENN CLARK

BOSTON

Little, Brown and Company

Twenty-ninth Printing

THE ATLANTIC MONTHLY PRESS PUBLICATIONS
ARE PUBLISHED BY
LITTLE, BROWN, AND COMPANY
IN ASSOCIATION WITH
THE ATLANTIC MONTHLY COMPANY

PRINTED IN THE UNITED STATES OF AMERICA

To the Inner Soul of America

In Appreciation

THERE are some modern-day prophets who hold that truth, like light, is impersonal, infinite, universal, and eternal, and who rejoice that they are selfless channels by means of which its radiance may reach humankind. The most exalted of these covet no personal fame for themselves, deriving their reward rather from seeing the dawn they love steadily expand and increase into high noon and flood all the plain with light.

From such Olympian light-gatherers as these I have lit my torch. The only acknowledgment I can conceive of that seems at all worthy of such pure natures is the continued spreading of their light, that it may reach a larger circle and bring joy to a greater number.

Only a few of these light-givers came to me in the form of books. More have come to me as friends bearing gifts; still more have come as eager questioners; their very needs have brought into the light new conceptions, which, had not their hunger drawn them forth, might otherwise never have been revealed. But deserving of gratitude above all the rest, a gratitude that can never be repaid in words, is that silent band of men and women of many churches and many creeds, whose prayers have been a mighty force in bringing into manifestation Truth more exalted than the voice of him who utters it, and Light greater than the lamp that sends it forth.

Contents

Contents

The Soul's Sincere Desire

The Soul's Sincere Desire

The Soul's Sincere Desire

I DO not know why God should have blessed me for the past three years with an almost continuous stream of answered prayer. Some of the answers were marvelous, many unexplainable, all of them joy-giving. But, greater than any particular blessing that came with any particular answer, greater than the combined blessings of all the combined answers was a gift, a blessing, that was so much larger, so much more inclusive than all the other special gifts that it encompassed all within itself. I refer to the peace and happiness and absolute liberation from the bondage of fear and anger and the life-destroying emotions that came to me and revealed to me the practicability of finding the Kingdom of Heaven in the practical world of men.

Concomitant with this great blessing came the impulse to share it with others — to pass it on that they too might have their burdens eased and their paths made smooth. But whenever I approached a friend to tell him how I prayed, my brain stumbled and words failed me. My method was so simple that it defied analysis. Like the air I breathed, it could not be captured and confined in any form.

So two years went by. Then one day, while walking home from college, a student said to me: "I wish very much that you would tell me how you pray. Won't you tell me sometime?" It suddenly occurred to me that this was the first time anyone had put that question to me. I do not know whether it is that every question has its own answer residing in it, just as every seed contains the entire life-plan of the completed plant; or whether the commands of Jesus, "Ask, and it shall be given you; seek, and ye shall find; knock, and it shall be opened unto you," were meant to be applied to questions we ask of each other as well as questions we ask of God when we do so in the spirit of Christian humility and love; but this I do know: late in the evening the answer to this question leaped full-fledged into my brain. For two years I had striven in vain to answer a question that no one had ever asked; and then in a twinkling, before a question asked in all sincerity and with honest purpose, the answer came.

The essay which follows contains the answer to that question. I wish to have it clearly understood, however, that I do not wish the method here described to become a formula. I offer it rather as an opening of doors and windows through which man's soul may find liberation from the confinement of the things which bind, and expand a bit to meet the ever-expanding love of God.

I find the frame for my method in the Lord's Prayer and the Twenty-third Psalm. I say "frame" because either one of these can be recited in less than half a minute, and a prayer such as we materialistically-minded moderns need is one which will demand at least fifteen minutes of our time.

In this day of the coliseum, the gymnasium, and the "daily dozen," I know it may sound impractical and visionary to suggest that the spirit deserves as much care as the body. But is not our spiritual health as important to our well-being as our physical health? Is not the life more than the food, and the body more than the raiment? Is not the kernel within the seed and the sap within the oak — in other words, that which is within, vitalizing, propelling the life processes — more important than that which is without and can be seen and touched?

Let me stand in the market place with the physical culturists and demand, as they demand, fifteen minutes of your time every day for two months. And while I hesitate to promise, as they promise, that at the end of that time you will find yourself a new man, this I can say: at the end of that time you will find yourself in a new world. You will find yourself in a friendly universe, where religion will no longer be a thing to be believed or disbelieved, a thing to be worn or cast off, but where religion will be a part of life as blood is a part of the body.

[5]

You will find yourself in a new world where your God no longer dwells in churches and meeting-places and forms and days, but where He governs every minute of every day of every year. You will find yourself in a new world where immortality will no longer be sought as something far away, to be found at some far distant time, for you will know that you are immortal now, and that the entire universe with all its good and with all its beauty belongs to you now and forever.

Let us take then, as our model, the zeal and steadfastness of the physical culturist, and utilize it in the field of the spirit. To associate these two fields in our mind will prove very helpful for our present purpose, for a prayer should be for the spirit exactly what calisthenics should be for the body — something to keep one in tune, fit, vital, efficient, and constantly ready for the next problem of life.

Now what are the underlying principles in Walter Camp's "daily dozen"?

1. The first principle is that the man shall stretch his muscles, as the caged lion stretches, whenever he can. And, mark you, the muscles that are seen are not so important as the muscles that are unseen — in the language of Walter Camp, "the muscles under the ribs." This should be the first principle of prayer also. One should first of all stretch the mind to take in God, not a one-sided,

two-sided, or a three-sided view of God, but *all*. Moreover, this stretching should not be for the objective mind — which is where we can see and control it — so much as for the subjective mind, the mind that is out of sight, the mind that is "under the ribs."

2. The next principle underlying the daily dozen, as well as all other good setting-up exercises, is to breathe deeply and freely. There is nothing that clears the brain and avenues of circulation like breathing with eleven elevenths of the lungs and not with one eleventh — breathing out the old waste poisons and breathing in the new clear life from the atmosphere which surrounds us. This should be the second step in our prayer. We should pray out the bad and pray in the good; dismiss from our mind the trouble which seems imminent and restate emphatically the great promises of God; forgive the sinner and accept forgiveness for the sin.

3. The final phase of these exercises is that they should be kept up steadily, daily, until the habit of deep breathing has been transferred to the nervous system; in other words until it becomes an automatic habit, so that a man between jobs at his office unconsciously stretches his legs under the table and continues all day to breathe deeply and freely from the depths of his lungs. This is

[7]

also the goal of all true prayer — to make the "stretching" of the mind to see God a continuous habit all through the day, to make the deep breathing of the soul — which mentally denies entrance of the bad thought to the brain and expands the good thought — a steady automatic habit of the subconsciousness. This is in accord with St. Paul's admonition, "Pray without ceasing."

As stated above, we find this "frame" suggested to us in the Lord's Prayer and the Twenty-third Psalm. The first phase — the expanding of the mind to take in all of God — is put very briefly in these short half-minute prayers; nevertheless, they were full of connotation for the ones to whom they were given. "The Lord is my shepherd." "Our Father Who art in Heaven, hallowed be Thy Name." Think of what the words "shepherd" and "Father" imply!

The second phase of prayer, the denial and affirmation, is suggested figuratively in the Psalm by "Thy rod and Thy staff," and the actual denials are given in very clear-cut form: "I shall not want," and "I will fear no evil." Each of these is followed by a series of affirmations. In the Lord's Prayer, this rhythmic handling of our problems is suggested by "Forgive us our debts, as we forgive our debtors." This suggests the in-breathing and out-breathing of that prayer which is real communion with God.

The third phase — that is, keeping the prayer-thought as a continuing force throughout the day — is suggested very beautifully in both the examples we are using: "Surely goodness and mercy shall follow me all the days of my life, and I will dwell in the house of the Lord forever"; "Thy Kingdom come, Thy will be done, in earth as it is in Heaven." You can see in these statements a realization of the Kingdom *here* and *now*, about us, in whatever activity we may be engaged.

How then shall we apply these principles to our own prayers? Perhaps some examples may help here. The following may open your eyes a wee bit to the possibilities you yourself might work out in prayer.

Stretching the Mind to Take in All of God

1. Our Heavenly Father, we know that Thy Love is as infinite as the sky is infinite, and Thy Ways of manifesting that Love are as uncountable as the stars of the heavens.

2. Thy Power is greater than man's horizon, and Thy Ways of manifesting that Power are more numerous than the sands of the sea.

3. Thy Wisdom is greater than all hidden treasures, and yet as instantly available for our needs as the very ground beneath our feet.

4. Thy Joy is brighter than the sun at noonday and Thy Ways of expressing that Joy as countless as the sunbeams that shine upon our path.

5. Thy Peace is closer than the atmosphere that wraps us around, and as inescapable as the very air we breathe.

6. Thy Spirit is as pure as the morning dew, and yet as impervious to all that is unlike itself as the diamond which the dew represents.

7. As Thou keepest the stars in their courses, so shalt Thou guide our steps in perfect harmony, without clash or discord of any kind, if we but keep our trust in Thee. For we know Thou wilt keep him in perfect peace whose mind is stayed on Thee, because he trusteth in Thee. We know that, if we acknowledge Thee in all our ways, Thou wilt direct our paths. For Thou art the God of Love, Giver of every good and perfect gift, and there is none beside Thee. Thou art omnipotent, omniscient, and omnipresent, in all, through all, and over all, the only God. And Thine is the Kingdom, and the Power, and the Glory, forever. Amen.

The Deep Breathing of the Soul

Before it is possible to breathe, one must be surrounded by atmosphere and atmosphere must *be in one*. Likewise, before it is possible to commune with God, which is a more conventional way of characterizing the deep breathing of the soul, one must know that God surrounds all and God is in all; that the Kingdom of Heaven is *here* and *now*.

As breathing is a mere rhythmic interchange of that which is within for that which is without, a casting-out of that which seems to be bad and a receiving, in its stead, of that which seems to be good, so the breathing of the soul is a casting-out of all that would poison, cramp, or belittle life — in short all that is *unlike* God, and a taking-in of all that is pure, perfect, and joyous, and which enriches life — in short, that which is *like* God.

Without question the very finest examples of this rhythmic communion with God are to be found in the Psalms of the Old Testament. And as our New England forefathers used to begin the day by offering a prayer and reading a Psalm, why can we not emulate their example and add to it perhaps just a touch of originality by offering a prayer and improvising a psalm? Indeed, is not the psalm as much a part of worship as a prayer, and is there any more reason why present-day worshipers should be limited to the collection of Psalms preserved for us in the Old Testament than that we should be limited in our prayers to the petitions preserved for us in Isaiah, Jeremiah, and the ancient Prophets?

The only new and revolutionizing idea that I am introducing into this discussion of prayer, in fact, is a plea for reinstating the psalm, the little brother of prayer, in our private and public worship. We find it now lost completely to our private worship and reduced to a mere form in our public worship. What I wish to see is the bringing of the psalm back in the form and manner that the old Psalmists themselves made use of, as a frank and spontaneous improvisation in the presence of a real need, an imminent calamity, a present sorrow — an actual outpouring of that particular need, trouble, or sorrow upon the outstretched arms of God, and the breathing in of His healing peace, comfort, and love. Such psalms were in themselves prayers — the finest and purest examples of prayer that the world has ever seen, of prayer which is dynamic and healing, of prayer which is a real communion with God.

As our first spiritual exercise of the morning was a stretching of the mind to take in God, so this is a breathing of the soul. And just as in physical breathing we give a quick expulsion of the poisons we wish to eliminate, and then drink in slowly of the new, fresh, life-giving, body-building ozone, holding it, first deep in the lungs, then high, turning it over, so to speak, till we have completely absorbed the life-giving oxygen, so we should give our denials with expulsive force, turning instantly to the constructive, soul-building affirmations. The trouble with most of our praying, as with our breathing, is that it is too negative. We shut ourselves up in a cramped little three-dimensional room with our negations, breathing in again and again the troubles that we should let vanish into thin air, instead of turning to new and fresh air — to God.

Marvelous results will come if one will turn in thought to God and Heaven, deny the existence in Heaven of the wrong thing felt or thought, and then realize that in God and Heaven the opposite condition prevails. One must dismiss from his mind completely the thought that the wrong thing felt or seen is permanent, and then follow instantly with the realization that the opposite condition exists here and now.

For money troubles, realize: There is no want in Heaven, and turn in thought to 1, 2, and 7 in Exercise I.

For poor health, realize: There is no sickness in Heaven, and affirm 1, 7, 6, 2, and 5.

For aid in thinking or writing, realize: There is no lack of ideas, and affirm 3 and 7.

For happiness: There is no unhappiness in Heaven, and affirm 1, 4, and 5.

For criticism and misunderstanding: There is no criticism in Heaven, and affirm 1, 4, 5, 6 and 7.

For friends: There is no lack of friends in Heaven, and affirm 1, 4, and 7.

For worry: There is no worry in Heaven, and affirm 4, 5, and 7.

This is the kind of prayer the Psalmists of old had recourse to in their hours of trouble — the most beautiful example of which is the Shepherd Psalm.

FIRST PHASE
The Lord is my shepherd

SECOND PHASE
I shall not want

He maketh me to lie down in green pastures,
He leadeth me beside the still waters.
He restoreth my soul.
He leadeth me in the paths of righteousness for his name's sake.

(Yea, though I walk through the
valley of the shadow of death)

I will fear no evil

For thou art with me.
Thy rod and thy staff they comfort me.
Thou preparest a table before me in the presence of mine enemies.
Thou anointest my head with oil.
My cup runneth over.

THIRD PHASE
Surely goodness and mercy shall follow me
All the days of my life,
And I will dwell in the house of the Lord forever.

Practising the Presence of God

And now, having finished the prayer which in form is something like a Psalm, and having finished the Psalm which is similar to a prayer, let us consider how we can turn the strength derived in the quiet hour into the daily routine of the world of action. For the test of every life is, after all, How do the hours of contemplation harmonize with the hours of action?

The value of Walter Camp's "daily dozen" is that after the fifteen minutes' exercise in the morning you find you are breathing a little deeper *all day*. We should expect the same results from our fifteen minutes of prayer every morning. We should be living in the Kingdom of God a little more vitally all day. How? Let me tell you.

Here is where we can learn a lesson from the movies. No longer does one have to depend upon newspapers for news; one can see the world's news thrown on the screen if one desires. Then why does one have to depend entirely upon one's prayers for contact with God? Cannot one see, if one knows how, the spiritual ideas of God revealed in the cinema pictures that flash by in actual life? The moment one awakes to the fact that one lives in God's world here and now, one begins to see in every event that comes a part of the beautiful symmetrical plan of

God. Of course, as it flashes by in little separate pictures of a fraction of a second each, not every picture may seem quite perfect. Neither would every stitch of a famous tapestry appear perfect to an eye looking through a microscope.

Once reach this stage and you have found the secret of following Paul's seemingly impossible command, "Pray without ceasing." And now miracles will begin to happen around you.

When a visitor comes, accept him as a messenger from God, and before long a divine message actually will come to you. Accept every disappointment as a signpost to show you to another path which is better, and you will always find the other path is there. Gradually this practising the presence of God, or living in the Kingdom of Heaven, will become a habit. Then you will wonder why for so many years you had not been living there before.

But remember that the best way to get there is to stretch the mind frequently to take in all of God that you can, and practise frequently the deep breathing of the soul. In other words, one can enter the Kingdom only by prayer and meditation. "Love the Lord thy God with all thy heart, and with all thy soul, and with all thy mind, and with all thy strength." "Seek ye first the Kingdom of God and his righteousness; and all these things shall be added unto you."

Thoughts about Prayer

Think of God and Heaven, not of the bad thing you are tossing off into the air.

Pray if possible out of loyalty to God, for the joy of it, not for results.

Do not pray to bring things to pass; pray to see things that are already in the Kingdom.

Do not limit the avenues by which God will answer your prayers. Remember that God's ways of manifesting His love are as uncountable as the stars of the firmament.

Do not feel responsible for your prayers or the answer to them. God alone is the planner and knows best. Love, rejoice, and be thankful for the unfoldment of His plan as you see it.

A Lost Art of Jesus

JESUS had a power of overcoming trouble, a power of triumphing over the "prince of this world," which was unique in the history of mankind. All will agree to this, even the skeptics and agnostics and those of alien faiths. Among the recorded promises which have come down to us as spoken from His lips was one that He would leave us this power: "Verily, verily, I say unto you, he that believeth on me, the works that I do shall he do also; and greater works than these shall he do; because I go unto my Father." Up to now the world in general and His professed followers in especial have failed, as a whole, to experience that power which He said He was going to leave with us. The question that is left unanswered is, What is that power which Jesus promised He was going to leave us, and where shall we find it?

Is Jesus' power of healing the sick, of bringing peace to the troubled, and harmony out of discord a lost art? Perhaps nothing in song or story is more alluring to the imagination than the so-called "lost arts." What were they, and where are they to be found? Like the riddle of the Sphinx or the oracle of Delphi, they remain shrouded in the veil of mystery which all the king's horses and all the king's men of modern scientific and philosophical research are powerless to uncover.

I have come to the conclusion that the greatest of all the lost arts — lost for these twenty centuries — is the great art of living as Jesus practised it: living in such a way that trouble fell like scales from the eyes of all those about Him who were in need.

If this art is lost, where shall we go to find it? For if it is truly the greatest of all the arts it is certainly worth the seeking.

Where does one go when he has lost something? Naturally he goes to the place where it was last seen, and makes that the starting-point for his search.

Let us take for an example what is probably the commonest of lost articles in this athletically ardent nation — the lost golf-ball. Just imagine you are caddying, say, for the greatest of all masters of the game. Stroke after stroke you have seen him drive down the course. Nothing equal to it have you ever seen before. And yet in spite of his marvelous power he does not require you to go on ahead, as a servant in his hire, but he invites you to accompany him at his side — as a companion. "I call you not servants," is the beautiful phrase of the Gospel, "I have called you friends." And oh, how you glory in this friendship and want to prove yourself worthy of this great trust! And then, in an evil hour, when you should have been giving your undivided attention to the game, you lose sight of the ball for just one moment and when you try to see it again in its onward flight you are not able to do so, and when you go down the course to seek it, try your very best, you cannot find it.

After wasting precious minutes threshing through the deep grass of inductive speculation on one side of the course, and searching among the high trees of deductive speculation on the other, and after poking in the sand traps of logic in the fairway, you are ready to give up in despair. But if you are a good caddy you still have one recourse left. You can return to the tee and take the same stand you saw the master take when he struck the ball, you can take the same grip upon the club, and you can give exactly the same swing which he gave, while you let your eye follow the course such a stroke would inevitably carry the ball. If you do this, and then follow the track which your thought has recharted for you, you will come right to the lost ball.

That is, figuratively speaking, exactly what I did. Having assured myself, beyond peradventure of a doubt, that Jesus meant us to take Him absolutely at His word when He said, "The works that I do shall he do also; and greater works than these shall he do," and having convinced myself that within Jesus' own life lay concealed the secret of doing these mighty works, I went back down the pathway of history to where Jesus stood before He sent the Christ Idea whirling down the ages. I went to where He stood; examined carefully, as best I was able, the way He took His stand upon this earth, the manner in which He gripped the great issues of life, the way He swung the full force of that matchless strength and harmony of thought in the great game of life; and then I let my eye follow the course which the Idea must have followed in its triumphant flight.

And this is what I found — that Jesus' attitude toward life was one of converting everything He saw and touched into parables. He stood on this earth as a symbol of a greater world. He gripped the issues of life as mere symbols of eternal and heavenly Realities. Petty problems and sorrows and disasters He converted into beautiful symbols of eternal and infinite goodness. Thus nothing was petty, nothing was trivial, nothing was without meaning in Jesus' world, for all things combined to reveal the King-dom — the Kingdom of Heaven in which He lived and moved and had His being.

"And in . . . parables spake he unto them . . . and without a parable spake he not unto them." Jesus was one above all others who never let His lips say what His mind and heart did not authorize. "Out of the abundance of the heart the mouth speak-eth." If Jesus talked in parables, He thought in parables; if He thought in parables, He felt in parables — the parable point of view of the universe was at the heart of His being. From somewhere about the beginning of His ministry He adopted this parabolic method of looking at the universe and thenceforth He never departed from it. There is something tremendously significant in this fact. It reveals that this method of thinking and talking about life for Jesus was not a halfway method. He did not use it occasionally as a means to an end, but continuously, exclusively, utterly. Perhaps no teacher in all history has so completely given himself to one particular method as Jesus did to this.

To me this was the greatest discovery of my life. It took its rank, in my little universe at least, beside Newton's and Watt's discoveries that apples fall downward and steam pushes outward. And I am firmly convinced that when the religious world as a whole awakes to the full significance and meaning implied in these simple words the result will be just as transforming to the spiritual life of the world as the discovery of gravitation and of steam power has been to the scientific and material life of the world. For just as the discoveries of Watt and of Newton awakened man to the presence of a new world of physical and material forces outside of him, so the discovery of Jesus' way of looking at life will awaken man to the presence of a new world of cosmic and spiritual forces within him.

Somewhere back in my memory I can recall seeing two books side by side on a library shelf, one entitled *The Parables of Our Lord* and the other entitled *The Miracles of Our Lord*. Either for this reason or for some other reason I early associated these two words as one would associate two companion-pictures that have hung on the wall in his childhood home, such as Sunrise and Sunset, the Parting and the Reunion, or those other heirlooms of our childhood memories — the dictionary and the family Bible that used to grace the centre table of the old living-room. But it was not till I made the discovery that I have just referred to that there came to me a realization of the deeper and closer association of cause and effect which existed between the parables and the miracles of our Lord. For in Jesus' parabolic interpretation of life actually lay the secret of the signs and wonders that signalized His healing and teaching ministry.

If all this is implied in Jesus' parabolic view of life, it behooves us to consider carefully just what manner of thing this mystery is that we call a parable — this thing that is so filled with moral and spiritual dynamite.

"A parable," says the dictionary at my hand, "is an allegorical relation of something real." There we have it: a parable deals first of all with Reality. Second, it translates this Reality in terms of the imagination. *Jesus looked at Reality through the lens of the divine imagination*. By means of that fact troubles vanished around Him, obstacles fell away, the lost became found, the sick became well, sinners became redeemed, and rough places became smooth. Moreover, He promised that those who followed Him and used the way He used should have similar dominion over all things on earth, and that greater works than He did should they be able to do also.

The imagination is the power we all possess of seeing harmonies, unities, and beauties in things where the non-imaginative mind sees nothing but discords, separations, ugliness. It is the tool of the mind with which we build up our affirmations — the "staff" of the Shepherd Psalm that comforts us when all other faculties fail us. To look at life imaginatively, then, to see everything about us as a great parable full of deep inner meanings — meanings of love, joy, wholeness, symmetry, and perfection — is to see life truthfully, that is to say, spiritually. It brings us into a condition of continuous prayer, a condition of cosmic consciousness, which is conducive, above all else, to bringing into our life those larger harmonies and unities that to our physical eyes appear to be miracles.

I am aware that I have here dug up from the ash-heap the stone which the theologians and the metaphysicians have for the most part rejected. And in setting it to be the head of the corner I know I shall meet with the scoffs and jeers of many who maintain that we should confine our attention to those things that can meet the test of logic and are capable of objective analysis. But the imagination is of all qualities in man the most godlike — that which associates him most closely with God. The first mention we read of man in the Bible is where he is spoken of as an "image." "Let us make man in our image, after our likeness." The only place where an image can be conceived is in the imagination. Thus man, the highest creation of God, was a creation of God's imagination. The source and centre of all man's creative power — the power that above all others lifts him above the level of brute creation, and that gives him dominion over all the fish of the sea, the birds of the air, and the animals that move and creep on the earth — is his power of making images, or the power of the imagination.

The imagination of man is but the window or door which, when thrown open, lets the divine life stream into our lives. When it is thus thrown open man is brought into a condition of consciousness which, for want of a better word, is called inspiration. This heavenly inspiration is what links man to the divine and brings into existence our poets, composers, prophets, mystics, seers, and saints. This is a power that Jesus Christ had and that lifted Him above all other men — a power that He, however, in His immeasurable compassion and His infinite humility, wished to bestow upon others and share with them, that greater works than He had done they might do also.

These works — these mighty works, these miracles, if you will — are the direct outcome of Jesus' converting everything that He saw into parables. And a parable, we find, is merely "an allegorical relation of something real." Looked at from this angle, the performing of a miracle is not such an impossible task. It consists merely of looking at Reality through the lens of the imagination, and then letting this parable, or imaginative way of looking at Reality, bring to pass that thing which is spoken of as a miracle.

And what is Reality? Reality, in the eyes of the practical man, is made up of cold, hard facts. And what are the hard, cold facts of life? As we look about us in this world what we see all too frequently are the quarrels, bickerings, unhappiness, unfaithfulness, treachery, covetousness, and materialism everywhere. These are facts of life. But what are facts? Fact comes from the word *factum*, meaning something that we do or make. Are these facts of life identical with the realities of life? Not according to Jesus. To Him Reality does not consist of that which is *made*, but of that which eternally *is*. *Love is* — quarrels are made; *joy is* — unhappiness is made;

truth is — lies are made; *loyalty is* — betrayals are made; *purity is* — impurity is made; *life is* — sickness is made. So Jesus went through life seeing no quarrels, no unhappiness, no lies, no impurity, no sickness. Where they appeared to be He turned the lens of His divinely inspired imagination upon them; He converted them into parables, and behold, they stood forth revealed as mere shadows or reflections — upside down — of the *reality*. And every time that Jesus converted a fact into a reality the people exclaimed that a miracle had been wrought.

Bear in mind I do not mean to imply that Jesus went about disregarding and overlooking the facts of life. Rather He looked at them so much more steadily, so much more understandingly than the rest of mankind that He *looked right straight through them* into the underlying Reality of which they were the mere counterfeits or reflections. This is what the parabolic point of view consists of. He looked steadily at the dead girl until He could utter with absolute conviction, based upon perfectly clear understanding, this startling parable: "The maid is not dead, but sleepeth." He looked through the palsied sufferer until He could pronounce with conviction another parable, "Thy sins are forgiven thee." For to Jesus a parable meant simply the going back behind the fact to the Reality that the fact represents. It does not mean watering the leaf that is waving conspicuously in the sunshine, but watering the roots that no one can see. It does not mean healing a man's skin, but healing his soul. It does not mean dealing with the seen, but with the unseen; not with the carnal, but with the spiritual. Once perform the inner watering, the inner cleansing, and the outer healing will follow as a matter of course. "Whether is easier, to say. . . . Thy sins be forgiven thee; or to say, Arise, and take up thy bed, and walk?"

And here let me pause a moment to clear up a misunderstanding in regard to the imagination that may have cropped up in the thought of many of my readers. There are some who have always thought that the imagination was something which makes believe that which is not. This is fancy — not imagination. Fancy would convert that which is real into pretense and sham; imagination enables one to see through the *appearance* of a thing to what it really *is*. Let me illustrate.

You who are reading this essay are probably sitting in a room with a perfectly flat floor beneath you. A carpenter, a contractor, and an architect brought their combined skill into action to see that the floor was flat — set level with the world. When you look out of the window, you very likely see the streets and gardens about you as also flat. For three thousand years — and perhaps far longer —all mankind believed the world was flat. Why?

Because they believed the evidence of their eyes. At last there came a man who looked at the world with his imagination, and he saw that it was round.

As you are reading you look out of the window and see the sun setting behind the western hills. You say the sun is going down. For thousands of years all mankind believed that this was so — in short, that the earth was the centre of the universe, and the sun, moon, and stars revolved around it. At length there arose a man who used his imagination sufficiently to see through the appearance of things to the Reality. Because he insisted that the sun stood still and the earth revolved around it — in short, tried to duplicate Joshua's miracle of making the sun stand still — his theory was regarded as a heresy.

Now did Columbus create a miracle by proving that the earth was round when all the kings and all the kings' men "knew" it was flat? And when he proved it was round did he actually make it round? No. It was round all the time — he merely demonstrated to mankind that it was round. Did Copernicus make the sun stand still and the earth revolve around it? No, he created no miracle — he merely demonstrated and proved what was actually so. And, like Jesus, "he marveled because of their unbelief."

And in like manner we may ask, Did Jesus perform a miracle when He said the leper was made whole? No, He merely demonstrated it. Did He break a natural law when He said, "The maid is not dead, but sleepeth"? No, He merely demonstrated that Life is the Reality, and Death is merely a shadow or counterfeit of Life.

Then can we create miracles? Yes, we can if we use our imagination and look steadfastly through appearances of things to the Reality behind them. We cannot create miracles by our fancy — by trying to make believe we see things that we do not and cannot see because they do not exist. We can create miracles by faith — by knowing the Reality that exists behind the things that only seem to exist. Faith will indeed move mountains.

And what is the greatest of all Realities, the Reality around which all lesser Realities centre, as it were? The Great Reality, the realization of which was at the core of all Jesus' miracles, was the truth that Man is eternally united with all that is good — in other words, with God and His Kingdom — and eternally separated from all that is bad. Merely to see this Reality and see it clearly enough will make the sick whole, the sorrowful happy, the sinful redeemed, and the lost found.

In the True Spirit

I come now to where all this has led me: If Jesus talked, thought, and felt in parables, He must also have prayed in parables. In other words, when He asked for physical and material blessings He must first have translated these needs into symbols of spiritual values and prayed not for the material facts but for the spiritual Realities which these facts represented. When He prayed for things that are seen He used the language of the unseen. Interesting evidence for believing that this is exactly what Jesus did is furnished us in some old records unearthed in Egypt, which contain a saying ascribed to our Lord: "Ask for great things, and the small things will be given unto you; ask for heavenly things, and the earthly things will be given to you." I can paraphrase this as follows: Seek spiritual values, and earthly things, expressing those values, will be given to you. Or, as Paul would put it: "Set your affection on things above, not on things on the earth." Which is simply to say in another way, "Seek ye first the kingdom of God, and His righteousness; and all these things shall be added unto you."

[31]

Let us apply this method of prayer to two of the commonest things in American life, two things that are quite generally thought to be so worldly and mundane that they fall outside the proper scope and field of prayer. I refer to our sports and our business. Here, if anywhere, we certainly agree that the parable method will be brought to its severest test. How can a man in either of these fields with any sense of propriety go to God in prayer unless he can first pass his desires through the filter of Jesus' parabolic vision and bring them forth purified of all dross and sediment of personal desire — that is to say, of Self? Imagine two rival athletic coaches both praying for victory. Imagine the presidents of two rival business firms praying for a monopoly of the trade in their line. How can either prayer be answered without disregarding, annulling, or violating the hallowed sanctity of the high office of prayer?

Just let us imagine a scene up in Heaven when two such conflicting prayers are received there. God gathers His angels together and says, "Down there are two earnest men asking for victories. Search through our stockrooms and our treasuries and gather together all the victories you can find and send them down to them." Presently the angels come back and report, "We don't find any such thing up here as victories. But we do find an old record which relates how an angel, the most beautiful of all those who sang before Thee, once made the request to be first in Heaven. If memory serves us right, Thou didst recommend that he journey down to a lower realm, where such requests might more appropriately be granted." Needless to say that the prayers of the two men, while not reproved in so emphatic a manner as was Satan, nevertheless remain unanswered.

Then how may one pray for athletic victories?

First of all by seeking the Reality back of the idea of victory. What is the real object of these contests? To improve the condition — physical, mental, and spiritual — of the men, and tone up the morale or condition of consciousness of the institution they represent. Will victory help this? It certainly will help it if achieved honestly and fairly, but it is in no wise indispensable or even essential. I find — by looking hard at Reality — that the physical condition of the men depends chiefly, not on the muscle fibre, but on the condition of the heart and the circulation of the blood. When I trace the heart back to its symbolical, that is to say, its parabolic meaning, — a meaning associated with it ever since the time of Homer, — I find it is the symbol of love; and likewise the circulation of the blood is the symbol of the circulation of joy through the consciousness. Love and joy for his athletic team are what the coach should pray for, not for victory. To summarize this briefly: —

To pray just for victory is bad — actually unmoral, if not immoral.

To pray for the team members to do their best is only a little better, for it leaves each member thinking of his own little "best," his own little personal responsibility to do his bit. It does not get back to the roots of things — to realities.

To pray for a condition of consciousness — a spiritual quality, not physical — that will enable an athlete to do his best is far better, as it goes down to the roots of things, to the Spirit, to the abiding trust that all are one body in Christ Jesus, and that all power comes from the Father.

This was all summed up by Jesus when He said, "Seek ye first the kingdom of God, and his righteousness," including love and joy, "and all these things," victory and self-expression, "shall be added unto you."

I had occasion to apply this truth last spring to a track team I was coaching, with amazing results; but, lest I clutter up this article with signs and wonders, I shall proceed to make clear the principles upon which it is based. For is not this method of prayer eminently logical and scientific? Do not physical scientists present to us situations that are analogous to this in their little outer universe of Time and Space?

Light, as we all know, comes to us from the sun. And yet scientists tell us that what comes to us as light is not light at all until it strikes the atmosphere that is wrapped about the earth. Then it suddenly breaks up into innumerable sunbeams, and we say that light is here. If anyone traveling through space should meet the sunbeams that are coming from the sun he would not recognize them as sunbeams. To him they would not appear as light at all, but as something else. Now let us imagine the people of this world getting together and deciding to petition the sun to send more light. They would send up a radiogram, "O Sun, send us more light!" The Sun would call together his servants and say, "The good people down below are asking for more light. Search all our stockrooms carefully, and if we have any on hand send it to them at once." So the servants of the Sun would hunt carefully and finally come to him and say, "We have searched far and wide and find no such thing as light. We find vibration, motion, all kinds of beautiful rhythms, but no such thing as light." Yet the people down below, in their blindness and ignorance, would continue to cry, "More light! Give us more light!" and the only answer they could receive is the comment of James, "Ye ask, and receive not, because ye ask amiss."

Indeed, I used this very illustration one day to a college president who had telegraphed me that he

was coming to talk about the problem of praying
for a large endowment campaign that was fraught
with immense possibilities, if it succeeded, as well
as immense peril, if it failed, to the college whose
destinies he guided. We were talking together in a
downtown hotel and I used the above illustration
as applied to money problems. Then I added: —

"You have a problem of raising many hundreds
of thousands of dollars. For many days you have
been thinking and living and praying in terms of
dollars. Let us stop and see just what these dollars
represent. Are they not ideas — ideas of culture,
inspiration, beauty, freedom, wisdom, and truth?
Have not men obtained such ideas seated on wooden
benches in country schoolhouses? Have they not
received them when seated on one end of a log with
a Mark Hopkins on the other? Have they not
received them while gathered on the shore, with
their Master seated in a boat? Ideas are really what
the world wants, what the students want, what you
want; and the thousands of dollars you need for
endowment, for buildings, for equipment, are merely
the means by which you would have these ideas
released in the largest possible way in order to do the
greatest possible good to the greatest number. I
know that if you could go back to Mark Hopkins on
one end of a log and a boy on the other you would
gladly do it. But as a matter of fact that would

require more money — not for the logs, but for a sufficient number of Mark Hopkinses to go around for the boys and the logs — than the actual money you are looking for now.

"At any rate you know and I know that the real thing you want is ideas, and not money. If one should pray to his Heavenly Father for money, what would happen? Suppose the Father should gather the angels about him and say, 'They seem to want money down below there. Look through our treasuries and our storehouses and find that which they seek and send it to them, for it is my good pleasure to grant every request of my children.' Presently the angels would return and report, 'We have searched all the inner treasuries of the Kingdom and we find no such thing as money. We have nothing up here that moth and rust can corrupt or that thieves can steal. All we can find are ideas — beautiful, glorious ideas — of abundance, of ease, of leisure, of service, of truth, of beauty. Shall we send them?' 'No,' the Lord might reply; 'wait until they ask for them.'

"Again the only answer they who are asking could receive would be the words of James: 'Ye ask, and receive not, because ye ask amiss.'

"But suppose we should ask, seek, and knock for spiritual ideas, and not for material things — what would happen? Simply this: that a veritable downpour of ideas — almost a hurricane or blizzard of ideas, if you please — would be shed down upon us, and as soon as these ideas struck the atmosphere of this earth they would — many of them, at least — be converted into good round hard practical dollars, the means by which these ideas of truth, culture, beauty, and happiness could be released in up-to-date colleges in this modern, complex, cosmopolitan age. For one thing we must give God credit. He has sometimes been accused of being a tyrant, and once — by the author of Job — of being a practical joker. But no one at any time has ever accused God of being an ignoramus or a fool. He knows our practical modern needs better than we do ourselves. Not until we set our affection on things above rather than on things of the earth will He grant the requests of His children.

"'When thou prayest, enter into thy closet, and when thou hast shut thy door, pray to thy Father which is in secret; and thy Father which seeth in secret shall reward thee openly.' "

And now I am called upon to answer a sensible and sincere question. Is there not a certain amount of hypocrisy and subterfuge in asking for one thing in secret, as it were, and desiring another thing to be given to us openly? In asking for ideas, for instance, and desiring money; in asking for love and joy, and desiring victory?

There is the very issue, my friend. As long as one asks for one thing and *desires* another his prayers remain unanswered. Not until the athletic coach has persuaded himself in his own heart that the pearl without price that he desires above all other things for his athletes is that they be filled to overflowing with love and joy, entirely regardless of whether victory or defeat shall accompany this love and joy, can he begin to see the real *power* that such love and joy can release in his men. Not until the college president genuinely desires first and foremost that actual ideas shall come to his college, if need be from teachers in homespun talking to boys on broken benches, and ceases to press down on the thought that these ideas must be presented in great million-dollar buildings and paid for by great million-dollar endowments, can he begin to see the real supply contained in *the spiritual idea* made manifest.

But how can I explain why so many petitions asked in the old way — without a parable — have been answered? Always for this reason and for no other: they were first translated — if not consciously in the mind, then unconsciously in the heart of the petitioner — into a parable. The petitioner was looking at the inner spiritual Reality and not at the outward material manifestation of Fact or Thing. In other words, such prayers were answered only when they were offered in simple trust and always

with that complete surrender to the will of God —
uttered or unexpressed — contained in the simple
words, "Not my will, but thine, be done." "Thy
will" — whether the seeker knows it or not — is
always the spiritual will, just as "my will" is always
the material will. Thus this simple statement,
when uttered from the heart and not from the lips
only, is a veritable Aladdin's lamp for converting
a petition for material things into a petition for
spiritual things. In other words, it grants to God
the privilege of substituting His will for ours — that
is to say, of translating our literal language of the
flesh into the parabolic language of the spirit, and
thus releasing the spiritual powers and forces so
that they may become manifest in whatever way
seems necessary to meet the need that our petition
contains.

What I am trying to make clear is that we must
pray *not so much in another language as in another
spirit*. I am convinced that Jesus Himself used
both the new spirit and the new language, as His
continuous use of the parable in both His thinking
and His speaking gives us good reason to infer.
Moreover, I am convinced that He has given us
good authority for following His example and using
the new language as well as the new spirit when He
said, "Neither do men put new wine into old wine-
skins: else the skins burst, and the wine is spilled,

and the skins perish: but they put new wine into fresh wine-skins, and both are preserved."

And this assurance I can offer to all those who are willing to give themselves to the Jesus method of prayer: You will find yourself lifted into a purer realm, where it will be easier to let the gross material of this earthly world drop from your consciousness, and where you can more easily give your thought, not to the Facts, which are *made*, but to the Realities, which are *not made, but eternal*. You will find yourself lifted into a rarer atmosphere where soon you will not be seeking for treasures upon earth, where moth and rust doth corrupt, and where thieves break through and steal, but you will be seeking — in language as well as in thought — for those treasures which are in Heaven, where neither moth nor rust doth corrupt, and where thieves do not break through nor steal. For where your language and your treasure are, there will your heart be also.

Greater than the prayer is the spirit in which it is uttered. Greater than speaking in parables, than thinking in parables, yes, even than praying in parables, is *living* in parables. This is the secret underlying the parable method of speech of Jesus — it is the parable method of living. He allied Himself spiritually — or, if you will, mystically — with the universe, just as a scientist allies himself with it mentally. And as a scientist talks of and about the great powers of nature that are unseen, Jesus lived, moved, and had His being knowing Himself to be one with the powers that are unseen, and gave expression to them in His life. He moved amid these spiritual forces with a grace and ease that are the marvel of the ages.

And this art — which He mastered in such a magnificent manner—upon the testimony of Jesus Himself can be ours if we are willing to pay the price: to take up our cross, follow in His footsteps, and look upon life as He looked upon it. And He looked upon life imaginatively — that is to say, spiritually. For the imagination sees things not in the flesh but in the spirit; not in imperfection but in perfection; not in ugliness but in beauty; not in discord but in harmony; not in parts but in wholes. Jesus came to make men spiritual, beautiful, harmonious, and whole. To that end He talked to them in parables, He thought for them in parables, He *prayed* for them in parables; "and without a parable spake He not unto them."

Now I come to that part of my message which is directed not primarily to the individual, but chiefly to those collective groups of religious bodies in this nation into whose keeping the divine fire of the Holy Spirit has been largely entrusted. And every word I speak is conceived in love, and every thought that goes out from me is born of prayer.

For I am like one who has been for a long while standing in an art gallery, shut away from the noisy world without. All around me hang the marvelous portraits and landscapes that Jesus has painted for us in His incomparable parables — pictures painted by the spoken word, conceived and colored in the depths of His divinely inspired imagination. Before me hangs the picture of the Samaritan, member of a despised race, bringing help and succor to one who had hated and despised him. Beside it hangs a picture of the righteous ruler, paying exactly the same recompense to all the workers in the vineyard, regardless of whether they represented faiths or creeds that had served him one hour or twelve. I see the prodigal and outcast son returning and being received into the open arms of a forgiving father. I see all about me the marvelous results of a Master Artist who has been painting pictures lovingly, patiently, conceived and inspired by an imagination great and broad enough to look out upon all types of humanity and have compassion upon them.

Having lived in this atmosphere of beauty, of harmony, of glory, I have become, like the Lady of Shalott, oblivious to things outside. But as I turn at last from this great, compassionate, harmonious, imaginative world that is within to the little world of chaos, discord, and logic that is without, when I lean far out the casement window and look around, what is it that comes into view to bring a catch in the throat and a dimness before the eyes? Far off down the winding ages I see Catholics who have no imagination burning Protestants; and Protestants who have no imagination burning Dissenters; and Dissenters who have no imagination burning Quakers; and Dissenters and Protestants joining forces to burn Catholics; and Jews burned and massacred by unimaginative Protestants and Catholics alike. And in the foreground we find Fundamentalists who have no imagination fighting Modernists who have no imagination, and one half of a congregation without imagination forming into a clique to quarrel with the other half formed into a clique, until one is tempted to raise his hands and exclaim: "If the blind lead the blind, shall not both fall into the ditch?"

The pity of it is that all these acts of the stunted, dwarfed, and crucified imagination, which bring discord, hate, and misunderstanding into the world, are done in the very name of Him who told the parables of the Prodigal Son and the Good Samaritan.

How can we account for this failure of the Christian Church to live up to the marvelous tenets of its Founder? Is it not because for centuries we have considered religion as a science — not as an art? Is it not because we have taught it in precepts and not in parables? Is it not because we have looked at it in the cold light of reason, and failed to live it in the warm light of imagination? Is it not because we have based our conduct upon the dogmas and creeds and formulæ of Aquinas, of Luther, of Calvin, of Jonathan Edwards, and not upon the simple parables of Jesus?

I am led to cry out: When, O men of the churches, were we told to cast out the imagination from our midst? Is it not time to take the stone which the builders have rejected and make it the head of the corner? Is it not time that we cease making of our religion a science merely, and make of it an art, as Jesus made it an art — an art of harmony, coöperation, sympathy, understanding, and brotherhood?

Strange it is that we have singled out and set apart the field of religion alone of all the branches of human activity for this glorification of science! In all other branches of human activity the art phase is stressed and the scientific basis considered subordinate. In business and in sports a man is not classified according to what he believes about a thing; he is classified according to the efficiency with which he does a thing.

What should we think of a golf-player turning to another and saying, "I am sorry, but you cannot play with me. I don't like your stance or the way you grip your clubs. This course is reserved for Presbyterians — you belong to the Baptists. You get over on your own course!" The actual test in golf is how far and how true a man can drive the ball. And *the only test in the art of religion, as contrasted with the science of religion, is how far a man can give his allegiance to the spiritual conception of the universe, and by his own life and conduct try to make the will of God prevail.*

Science talks *of* and *about* God, of and about Love, of and about Joy, of and about Peace, Truth, Wisdom, Purity, Harmony. Art *expresses* God, Love, Joy, Peace, Truth, Harmony, and Wisdom. Science investigates and correlates, unifies and explains life's great affirmations; Art grows into, becomes one with, and expresses life's great affirmations. A man may learn the laws of a science in a day; he can grow in an art for all eternity.

There may be many disagreements over the laws or methods underlying an art, but there is only one test of the art itself — does it get results? In the realm of science there may be as many hypotheses as there are scientists; in the realm of art there can be but one test: *does it manifest itself in life?* Does the orator make you weep, make you laugh, make you act? Then don't ask what theory of elocution he used. Did the boat's crew win the race? Then don't ask what theory of stroke they used. Did the picture smite you with beauty? Then don't ask what was the school of painting it represents. Did the good man throw open the windows for you and let God's blessed Spirit enter and fill your home? Did he make you realize you are a spiritual being living in a spiritual universe? Then don't ask what is his creed or to what church he belongs. Don't ask what mansion he lives in, for in our Father's house are many mansions. Suffice it to know that he belongs to the Father's house; that he lives in the consciousness of God's all-pervading Presence; that in God he lives and moves and has his being.

Brother Lawrence, that sweet-souled Catholic, was one who practised the presence of God as it was rarely given to man to practise it. Phillips Brooks also, in another age and another environment, lived the God-conscious life. The science, the "ology," the technique of their methods differed, and yet the results were the same. By their fruits they were brothers. Had they lived in the same age, in the same city, they would undoubtedly have found each other out — they would have become comrades in heart and partners in bringing the Kingdom of Heaven into the community where Providence had brought them together. Would that we had more like them to-day!

Could the Allies ever have won the war if Frenchmen had refused to fight in the same sector with Englishmen, and Belgians had refused to fight side by side with Americans? It was not until all united in harmony, in spite of the fact that each naturally represented a different theory or creed of military training and discipline, that the successful outcome of the World War was possible. And I prophesy that not until Catholics, Christian Scientists, Methodists and Unitarians, Fundamentalists and Modernists, can forget the differences underlying the science of their creeds and unite in the common cause of *living their religion* — that is to say, practising the art of living in allegiance to the spiritual conception of the universe — may we hope to see the power of Mammon broken and the victory achieved that will bring peace on earth and good will to men.

A Lesson in Prayer

PRAYER is governed by the same laws that govern the growth of the flower in the crannied wall; it is controlled by the same laws that control the flow of a stream, the art of a game, the life of a bee. For as God is in all things, so are His laws prevailing in all things; and as God is the same yesterday, to-day, and forever, so are His mighty laws the same yesterday, to-day, and forever. As prayer is life raised to its highest degree, so the laws of prayer are the laws of life raised to their highest expression. A man who learns and practises the laws of prayer correctly should be able to play golf better, do business better, work better, love better, serve better. For to learn how to pray is to learn how to live.

And to make this lesson very intimate, simple, practical, let us learn how to pray as we would learn how to play golf — naturally, joyously, as a part of the day's happiest experience. Let us go away from our lesson in prayer refreshed and unselfconscious, as we would go home from a golf game, an auto trip, or a fishing-excursion. I would that we might feel such complete freedom from all restraint that we should find ourselves talking about it easily, spontaneously — yes, enthusiastically, over our tea-cups, at the club, on street corners, in hotel lobbies, just as we would talk of any other interesting and natural experience of life. For it is the same, or should be the same, as all our other vital experiences, with this one difference, that there will be a quality of reverence surrounding it, greater perhaps than in the average experience, but a reverence that is such a part and parcel of our genuine selves that it can find its most appropriate and natural expression in simple, glowing enthusiasm and eagerness to serve rather than in timid reticence, silent withdrawal, and stern asceticism.

For the art of prayer, as we are going to learn it, derives its inspiration from the baptism of Jesus — not from the baptism of John. For John, you remember, "came neither eating nor drinking, and they say, He hath a devil. The Son of Man came eating and drinking, and they say, Behold a man gluttonous, and a winebibber."

For prayer, as Jesus saw it, was not a withdrawal from life and a fasting from the good things that life affords. It was a glorious taking-in of the completeness, the fullness of life; an actual hunger, if you will, for those infinite riches of the Spirit that, when properly understood, often result in surrounding one with good things on this earth as well — especially those good things which Macbeth, after he had lost the power to pray, felt he had forfeited: "honor, love, obedience, troops of friends." And where on this earth can be found riches more precious than these?

So I invite you, my friend, to join with me in a little game of golf. Leave the book unopened, the letter unanswered, the business unattended to. Those who think that the book, the letter, and the business must have the first attention should be reminded that all these things will be made much easier after they have come for a while further into God's out-of-doors, where the day is full of sunshine and the night is full of stars.

And what shall you bring with you to this game? Merely the willingness to give your attention, your thought. In other words, be sure to bring your brain bag with its neat assortment of clubs, those marvelously constructed powers and capacities constructed by the great Manufacturer, the Creator of all things. Bring besides a purpose, round and smooth and hard, which you would like to drive down the course of life toward ultimate success. A bag of clubs and a ball, a set of capacities and a wish — these are all that the game requires.

And now we have arrived at the starting-point. The first thing to do is to tee-up your ball, ready for the first stroke. A great box of sand tempts you to overdo this job, and if left alone your first mistake will be to half-bury your ball in the sand. Lest you do this, let me tell you what this sand represents: it represents trouble. Not until you have driven your ball into a sand bunker some day and wasted a dozen strokes trying to get it out will you realize the full significance of the truth I am telling you. But in the meantime take my word for it and use this sand carefully, sparingly, that is to say, scientifically. Make it serve you, not crush you. Just as a flag cannot grow without mire nor a reed without water, neither can one start a game of golf without sand nor a life of prayer without trouble. After a man gets out on the fairway he does not always have to use trouble to raise and sharpen his stroke; but, strange as it may seem, I have never seen a man make an efficient start in a life of prayer without having, first of all, to tee-up his purpose upon a little mound of trouble. Trouble is actually one of the greatest blessings that can come to a man who wishes to learn the game aright, provided he knows how to use it and not let it use him.

With the sand you make, as I said before, a tee. When properly made we call this tee a "lie." Use your imagination, your parable method of looking at life, — as you have learned in an earlier chapter, — and convert your trouble, or tee, into a lie. And remember that the more sand you find in the box, the better the lie you will be able to make, which means the better the start you will be able to make in your

game. Now, having picked your best driver, you are
ready to learn the big rules of the game.

The first rule you must heed is: "Don't top the
ball." The instinct that leads you to do this is the
grandfather of all the troubles of golf-playing. It
is the instinct to draw the club up to yourself. It is
the intrusion of the little self-thought into a great
and ancient game that began long before you were
born and will continue long after you are gone.

You may have smiled years ago when you read in
Rostand's *Chantecler* how the pompous little cock
thought that the sun's rising each morning awaited
his summons. You may now smile again when you
top the ball, for it manifests the same exaggerated
illusion of self intruding into your golf stroke.

This intrusion in prayer expresses itself in the ever
recurring question: "What does this mean to me?
What glory, what gain shall I get out of it?" One of
the reasons for Jesus' extraordinary power is traceable
directly to the complete overthrowing of this insidi-
ous temptation in the Wilderness at the very beginning of His public ministry. Later He gave powerful
and uncompromising utterance to the law which was
revealed to Him in that hour, when He said: —

> And when thou prayest, thou shalt not be as the
> hypocrites are; for they love to pray standing in the
> synagogues and in the corners of the streets, that they
> may be seen of men. Verily I say unto you, They
> have their reward.

The classic example of the man who hesitated to take the self-thought out of his dealings with God was Jonah, and to this day, when a message is laid upon us to deliver to our fellow men, we have our choice — to become a Jonah or a Moses, that is to say, to make ourselves a barrier or a channel. It was not until Jonah was willing to sacrifice self, even to the extent of being cast into the raging sea of annihilation, that he ceased to be a "Jonah," in the figurative sense, and became a saviour of men.

In contrast, note what a selfless channel Simon Peter was from the first moment that Jesus called him to become one of the fishers of men. Nowhere is this more forcefully brought out than in that Gospel which many commentators believe that Peter dictated to Mark during a sojourn in Rome. Only twice in the four Gospels is there a record of Jesus' pronouncing eulogies upon mortal men — one was upon John the Baptist, the other was upon Peter. The first was recorded in detail by the amanuensis of Peter, but the second, that which more than anything else must have made Peter's heart swell with joy, he withheld from Mark's gospel. On the other hand, the rebuke which Jesus gave Peter when he would have dissuaded Jesus from submitting to His appointed suffering, and the warning he received by the first crowing of the cock, were given in their entirety by Mark.

This modesty, which prompted the elimination of all personal allusions that would tend to glorify the writer, was characteristic of all the other inspired Gospel writers. An example of this is Matthew's conspicuous failure to mention the banquet he gave to Jesus immediately after he had been called, although the other Gospel writers deemed it important enough to be given a prominent place in their immortal records.

That their own Master was the purest example of this beautiful freedom from all personal vanity may be gathered from the following utterances: "I can of mine own self do nothing." "The Son can do nothing of himself, but what he seeth the Father do." And again, "Why callest thou me good? There is none good but one, that is, God." The Gospel records are full of such utterances.

This modesty or subordination of the little I or self to the great I AM, or God, is characteristic of all the writers of that great book, the Bible. Perhaps it is partly due to the anonymity of the writers that one has said, "The Bible comes out of profounder depths of human experience than any other book."

The time may be past when anonymity shall be a virtue in poets, historians, and dramatists; but the time will never be past when the impersonal, selfless prayer will not hold power over the egotistical, self-seeking prayer. Let us take care lest we, in the very midst of the most unselfish work for the most unself-ish causes, may not find ourselves one day praying the prayer of the Pharisee in the temple, forgetting that the simple, selfless prayer of the publican is more acceptable at the throne of Heaven. Rather than that such a thing should happen, let it be said of us as it was of Jesus by the railers before the Cross: "He saved others; himself he cannot save."

The next two rules are so allied to the first, as well as to each other, that they must be introduced with one breath. They are: "Don't pull the stroke, and don't slice the ball." If you pull the stroke the ball will curve in one direction and become lost in the high trees of Anger at one side of the course. If you slice the ball it will curve in the other direction and be lost in the high grass of Worry at the other side of the course. Both these "don'ts" are so closely related that we might say they are the lineal children of the inhibition that rises from the thought of self.

If this is true of golf, how much more true it is of prayer. Anger and worry, those twin offspring of the thought of self, have blocked more prayers, ruined more churches, retarded more the spiritual develop-ment of the race than all the other vices put together. Anger is a sign that we do not love God, for "inas-much as ye have done it unto one of the least of these, my brethren, ye have done it unto me." Worry is the sign that we do not trust God, or that we ascribe more power to something else than we do to God. Anything which affects the flow of love and trust toward God blocks the perfect flow of prayer. Jesus was particularly outspoken in his denunciation of both these sins.

A man once said to me, "I wish that when Jesus gave the Lord's Prayer to his disciples, he had added a footnote, telling them how to give it." As a matter of fact, that is exactly what Jesus did. This is his footnote: —

> For if ye forgive men their trespasses, your heavenly Father will also forgive you. But if ye forgive not men their trespasses, neither will your Father forgive your trespasses.

Is it not a striking fact that the only comment He made on this prayer was to the effect that it would work perfectly, provided the one who gave it had first rid himself completely of every unforgiving thought toward his fellow men, and that it would not function at all unless he did so purify himself.

In another place, when speaking of anger, He restated the same thought in different words: —

> Therefore if thou bring thy gift to the altar, and there rememberest that thy brother hath aught against thee; leave there thy gift before the altar and go thy way; first be reconciled to thy brother and then come and offer thy gift.

Thus we see that when Jesus discussed prayer in this immortal sermon He ended it with the emphatic injunction that anger must be absent from it; and when He discussed anger he stated emphatically that it must never be taken with the gift of prayer to the altar. From whichever angle he approached these two subjects he never neglected to make it plain that anger and effective prayer, like water and oil, could never mix.

If anger, that is to say, "hating God," blocks the perfect prayer, then worry, or "doubting God," is almost equally inimical to the perfect effect of prayer. Jesus' clarion call for perfect trust, which stands as the climax to the great Sermon on the Mount, is too fixed in our memory to require repetition here. Suffice it to say that the opening sentence should be emblazoned in every schoolroom and in every church until all who doubt God learn to trust Him: — "Be not anxious."

That John, the beloved disciple, considered fear one of the major sins is evidenced from the fact that he placed it first when enumerating the sins that separate man from God: —

> But the fearful, and unbelieving, and the abominable, and murderers, and whoremongers, and sorcerers, and idolaters, and all liars, shall have their part in the lake which burneth with fire and brimstone: which is the second death.

John was especially the disciple of love, and he held that love and fear could not abide together. He says, "Perfect love casteth out fear." He might have added, "Absolute fear casteth out love." Without love we cannot have perfect prayer. James also adds his word concerning the impossibility of combining fear and prayer on the altar of God: —

> But let him ask in faith, nothing wavering. For he that wavereth is like a wave of the sea driven with the wind and tossed. For let not that man think that he shall receive any thing of the Lord.

If we begin a prayer with fear in our hearts and end with fear totally gone, completely annihilated, we may rest assured that our prayer is answered — if not in our way, at least in God's way. If when we end our prayer our fear remains, we may know then that our prayer is not yet answered, and that more and purer prayer is needed. Often we are confronted with situations from which there appears to be no extrication, and from which it seems impossible that fear should be banished. But remember that Jesus has many times repeated His miracle of stilling the tempest, and can do it within the night of our heart just as easily as He did it in the night of Galilee.

How can we have this perfect trust? By knowing that every need has its own fulfillment, just as every seed has its own fruition; by using Jesus' parable method, and looking through the need to the reality it represents. When we plant a grain of corn we do not then stick a stalk into the ground above it. For the stalk comes out of the seed — from within it, never from without. Wait upon the Lord, and in His own way, in His own good time, we shall see the harvest issue from the need, just as the farmer sees the full-grown wheat come from the seed. Or we can think of ourselves as the little child described by Phillips Brooks: "The little child digs his well in the seashore sand, and the great Atlantic, miles deep, miles wide, is stirred all through and through to fill it for him." In the same way, in the presence of our human need all the divine forces in the universe are stirred through and through to fill it for us. Let us give ourselves up to such thoughts as this, knowing that around us are forces more fitted to take care of us than we ourselves. Let go, and know that God reigns and we are in His hands.

But these first three rules stated in the form of don'ts are not merely negations; they teach a lesson that is also constructive, affirmative, upbuilding. These three don'ts are don'ts of purification. We are taught in our grammar lessons that two negatives make an affirmative. In this case we may say that three negatives make one great affirmative — Be free! Be free for what? Be free to see God. When Jesus said, "Blessed are the pure in heart: for they shall see God," He meant more than an arid asceticism; He had in mind more than a rule of conduct compounded chiefly of negatives; He meant rather a whole cleansing of the soul, a removal of all débris which would obstruct the clear flow of God's will. We must first remove all the beams and motes of Self, with its vanity, covetousness, and egotism; of Anger, with its brood of jealousies, envies, and fault-finding; and of Worry, with its children of fear and cowardice; and after this cleansing we can turn the strong, clean, crystalline lens of the soul upon the infinite riches of Heaven and see them as they are in all their majesty, beauty, and glory.

Merely to see these riches is to possess them. Merely to see God is to have Him. In short, to see with the lens of the purified soul is to possess that which we see. This kind of seeing is infinitely higher than thinking. Spiritual seeing means spiritual possession. One who sees — that is, one who possesses in his soul — is one whose prayers are answered. This is verified by the custom that has come down to us from ancient times of calling the man whose prayers are answered not a thinker, but a seer.

These three don'ts, then, are not don'ts that bind; they are don'ts that liberate; and liberation is anything but negative. They make the way straight for the message of God to come to us. If we expect to get a message from the Father of Love we must see that the receiving apparatus is pure and vibrant with love. Any unloving thought clogs the flow of God's love, just as rusty pipes retard or prevent the even flow of life-giving waters from the great reservoirs in the mountains.

The first step, then, in preparing ourselves for prayer, is the clearing of the channel, making ready for the inflow of God's love. This is best done not by thinking of one's self, but by fixing one's eyes on God. Think of Him as ALL LOVING, ALL POWERFUL, ALL PERFECT, with no anger and no distrust and no fear. Then, keeping your gaze steadily upon Him, feel the petty annoyances, the prejudices, and the selfish desires falling away like worthless garments. Remember that every residue of wrong thinking, of malice, or of selfishness in your heart or brain clogs the reception of the downpouring light of love. Wipe from the glass of your vision the mist of self, and as Paul says, you will cease to see through a glass darkly and see face to face.

In His Name

AFTER a golfer has taken his stance, and has addressed the ball, when he has completely rid himself of the inhibitions of nervousness, impatience, and fear, when his wrists are relaxed and supple, ready to respond to his slightest command, then he is ready at last to give the stroke.

If you have seen a great golfer play you have seen one of the most wonderful things in the world, which, if it could be wholly analyzed and accounted for, would explain and elucidate the whole mystery of power and skill. After he has finished his preliminary relaxation of arms and hands, the great golfer rests in a quietness and confidence which he himself does not wholly understand, feeling only that there are powers far beyond him, which are ready and waiting to play the game for him. For he knows that he could never have learned how to play the game as well as he has done in three months, or three years, or even thirty years. He knows down in the deeper cells of his being that the marvelous coördination of mind and muscle that are his could not have been attained in one or even two or three lifetimes. He knows that the mighty rhythms and coördinations of eye and muscle and brain have been worked out for him through the history of the race. He, with his little body hardly out of swaddling clothes, with his little growth of muscle and bone and tissue that has seen the light of day for only a few revolutions of the earth, merely brings into use, with what direction and control he is capable of, the physical and psychic forces that are as old as Time. He knows that, when he sends the ball down the course with one of those perfect and majestic drives, he, as the small self, does not strike that ball, but all his ancestors rise and gird themselves and strike it for him.

In the same way the man who prays with power knows that he does not do the praying; he merely directs, in a very small and sometimes awkward way, forces that are greater than himself. Just as the great golfer is indebted to his physical heritage, the man who prays is indebted to the vast spiritual heritage of the race. The golf-player, made in the image and likeness of his physical father, plays with the instincts and physical prowess which his physical father has handed down to him. The man who prays, made in the image and the likeness of his spiritual Father, prays with the power, radiance, and glory given him from the spiritual powers of his Father, drawn from all the spiritual forces of the infinite universe.

This is the way Jesus prayed, and it is the reason all His prayers were answered. "The words that I speak unto you I speak not of myself," Jesus said, "but the Father that dwelleth in me." He reiterated to his followers that they must practise prayer in the same way. Seven different times He gave His disciples a promise the purport of which was, "Whatsoever ye shall ask the Father in my name, he will give it you." Jesus never spoke what was not true, and when He took the pains to repeat this seven times he surely meant that His word be heeded. I do not know of any other statement of Jesus which has been so misinterpreted or disregarded by most of his followers for the past two thousand years. And this in spite of the fact that He uttered it in such impressive fashion, followed it with examples and parables, and reiterated it so many times.

Now what does it mean to pray in Christ's name? Does it mean to pray in our own name, adding at the end a lame apologetic postscript that the prayer was offered in Christ's name? This smacks too much of cleaning the outside of the platter while within all is uncleanliness. It reminds me of my little girl, who, with a drawing that looked like a washtub, asked her mother to write upon it, "This is a kitty."

Jesus does not ask for labels — He asks for the real thing. He does not ask for prayers with clean exteriors only — they must be clean within as well. He does not ask that we pray in our own name and then add a hypocritical postscript: "In Christ's name I ask this."

Is it any wonder that our prayers have been so ineffective? All these years we have not been praying as Jesus told us to pray, in genuine communion with God, but have been trying to palm off on Him makeshifts, substitutes, and flimsy imitations.

"The 'name' in primitive thought stands for the person bearing that name; it is, in a sense, the person himself," writes Dr. H. Clay Trumbull. When a woman marries a man she takes his name — unless, as in some parts of the world, he takes hers — and the wife thereby becomes his possession, his representative. When she speaks in the assembly her voice becomes his voice. Jesus himself said, "And they twain shall be one flesh." To pray in Christ's name we should become one with Him — not in the flesh, but in the spirit.

A very beautiful custom in some parts of the South Sea Islands is that when two men become deeply attached to each other they exchange names, and each is known by the name of the other for the rest of his life. Such an exchange of names, — one speaking in another's name, — whether in marriage or in friendship, implies a sacred tie of absolute unity, absolute love. To speak in Christ's name then means that we love Him; we represent Him and express Him; we abide in Him and He abides in us.

"If we would ask anything in the name of Jesus," continues Dr. Trumbull, "we must first be sure that we are ourselves in that name, our life being hid in His life, our name in His name. . . . Coming thus to the Father, we come in the name, in the spirit, and in the likeness of His Son; and the Father will hear us and will answer us, because we are representatives of His Son, enwrapped by and dwelling within His very self as the supreme representative of the Father."

We might say that Jesus by a mere change of a preposition has revolutionized the entire conception of prayer. In the Old Testament days prayer consisted largely of offering sacrifices on an altar — an exhibition *before* God. In the New Testament it became a petition addressed *to* God. Jesus went one step further by using prayer as a communion *with* God. This change is very important. A writer says, "True prayer is, by our Lord's own witness, revealed to be not praying for God, or even to God, but with Him. . . . Strictly to state the truth, it is the Holy Ghost praying through and with us; for whilst 'we know not what we should pray for as we ought . . . the Spirit itself maketh intercession for us.'"

True prayer, then, is the Holy Ghost, Emmanuel, God in us, speaking through us to God the Father, Who abides in us and in Whom we abide. We are but the chosen vessel by means of which the living water is being carried from the spring to the sea. As breathing is merely a taking in and giving out of air, so prayer is merely a taking in and giving forth of God.

Is it any wonder that this kind of prayer is always heard, is always understood — *and is always answered?* For if God could hear and answer every prayer asked by God the Son, speaking through Christ in Galilee, cannot He hear and answer every prayer asked by God the Holy Ghost, speaking through Man to-day?

As the great golfer stands poised, with club above his head, ready for his mighty stroke, he knows he deserves no credit for the wonderful coördination of mind and muscle that is his. He knows that the mighty rhythms and unities and powers that are in him have been worked out for him by his earthly fathers from the beginning of the race. In a similar way the one who prays in Jesus' name knows that he deserves no credit and is not responsible for the mighty coördinations of mind and spirit that are his. He knows that the mighty rhythms and unities and powers in his heart and soul have been worked out by his spiritual Father from the beginning of the ages. He knows that all he needs to do is to release himself from the things that bind and relax himself completely to these mighty powers, and they will perform many mighty works through him.

The novice in golf who cannot give himself to the perfect stroke with its perfect "follow through," but who relies instead upon the "chop stroke" that begins and ends with self, can never hope to break a record. So the man who neglects the great unities and harmonies within him and prays a prayer that begins and ends with self must never expect to receive an answer to his prayer. For just as the golf player must give himself wholly and unqualifiedly to the instincts of the race, the man who truly prays must give himself wholly and unqualifiedly to the inspirations of Heaven.

Now we come to the most essential of all the laws of prayer: there must be Love in it. Paul said: —

> Though I speak with the tongues of men and of angels, and have not charity, I am become as sounding brass or a tinkling cymbal.
>
> And though I have the gift of prophecy and understand all mysteries, and all knowledge, and though I have all faith, so that I could remove mountains, and have not charity, I am nothing. . . .
>
> Charity never faileth: but whether there be prophecies, they shall fail; whether there be tongues, they shall cease; whether there be knowledge, it shall vanish away.

And he might have added: And though there be prayers, they shall fail; but if love be in the prayer it shall not fail.

Jesus wrought not a single miracle where He did not first love, and where the love was not returned unto Him. The greater the miracle the greater the love. He cared for the people who waited in the wilderness to hear Him. "I have compassion on the multitude," He said, "because they continue with me now three days and have nothing to eat: and I will not send them away fasting, lest they faint in the way." Before He healed the widow's son at Nain He saw her and "had compassion on her." Before He raised Lazarus from the dead He wept, and those standing by said, "Behold how he loved him!"

Nothing reveals better how perfectly Jesus abided by this principle that love be made the centre and core of prayer than His refusal to help the Syrophœnician woman who, having "heard of him," besought Him to cast out the devil from her daughter. Note the coldness of those words: having "heard of him." She was evidently coming to Him as to a necromancer, a foreign wonder-worker, a mysterious Jew. "But he answered her not a word." This manner of Jesus was similar to His manner with Pilate and the Jewish accusers; where there is no love Jesus is silent. When His disciples begged Him to send her away He answered, "I am not sent but unto the lost sheep of the house of Israel." Then to her, when she besought Him, He said that it was not meet to take the bread of the children — who love — and cast it to the dogs — those who do not love. Then in one of the most beautiful expressions of humble devotion and trust ever recorded she cried: "Truth, Lord: yet the dogs eat of the crumbs which fall from their masters' table."

Then Jesus answered and said unto her, "O woman, great is thy faith: be it unto thee even as thou wilt." And her daughter was made whole from that very hour.

The entire philosophy of Jesus' emphasis upon love as the key to healing men physically, mentally, and spiritually is revealed in a conversation that took place in the house of a Pharisee.

And one of the Pharisees desired him that he would eat with him. And he went into the Pharisee's house and sat down to meat.

And, behold, a woman in the city, which was a sinner, when she knew that Jesus sat at meat in the Pharisee's house, brought an alabaster box of ointment,

And stood at his feet behind him weeping, and began to wash his feet with tears, and did wipe them with the hairs of her head, and kissed his feet, and anointed them with ointment.

Now when the Pharisee which had bidden him saw it, he spake within himself, saying, This man, if he were a prophet, would have known who and what manner of woman this is that toucheth him: for she is a sinner.

And Jesus answering said unto him, Simon, I have somewhat to say to thee. And he saith, Master, say on.

There was a certain creditor which had two debtors; the one owed five hundred pence and the other fifty.

And when they had nothing to pay, he frankly forgave them both. Tell me therefore, which of them will love him most?

Simon answered and said, I suppose that he to whom he forgave most. And he said to him, Thou hast rightly judged.

And he turned to the woman, and said unto Simon, Seest thou this woman? I entered into thine house, thou gavest me no water for my feet; but she hath washed my feet with tears, and wiped them with the hairs of her head.

Thou gavest me no kiss: but this woman since the time I came in hath not ceased to kiss my feet.

My head with oil thou didst not anoint; but this woman hath anointed my feet with ointment.

Wherefore I say unto thee, Her sins, which are many, are forgiven; for she loved much: but to whom little is forgiven, the same loveth little.

And he said unto her, Thy sins are forgiven.

And they that sat at meat with him began to say within themselves, Who is this that forgiveth sins also?

And he said to the woman, Thy faith hath saved thee; go in peace.

Had Jesus turned the power of His miracles of compassion and love into a means of glory for His own fame, He would have become a wizard, a worker in black magic, a scourge instead of a Christ. The temptations to which Satan submitted Him were temptations to use the power of prayer divorced from love, in hypnotism, personal magnetism, and clairvoyance, for selfish ends, for personal glory. That such a temptation is a real one is evidenced by the histories of religious leaders who have lost their way, let love drop from their prayers, and let the self in. Such men make prayer a mere system, a mechanical routine, a formula. Whenever this happens, the power that before was kept alive by love is atrophied, and miracles cease to happen. Then prayers are no longer answered.

This actually did happen in the early Christian Church after it had become a State religion, a formal instrument of worldly elements. For three hundred years after Christ, according even to such an agnostic historian as Gibbon, the early Christians continued to work miracles, many of which were almost as great as those of Jesus Himself.

When congregations come together to pray, not merely to listen to a sermon or to go through a ritual, when love lives in the prayers and self is forgotten, then we may expect miracles again: for the blind to see, the lame to walk, and those possessed of fear and terror to be set free from demons.

The prayer without love is a cursed prayer, in league with the devil. Jesus repudiated such prayer at the beginning of His ministry, and again near its close He gave one final and blasting repudiation in the manner of the parable of the fig tree, which few are able to understand. The fig tree in Palestine does not bear leaves until after it has borne fruit. One day Jesus came upon a tree that was abundantly covered with leaves without having first borne its fruit. Jesus did what was for Him a strange thing; He, the soul of forgiveness and tenderness, cursed the fig tree. When He and His disciples passed it again they found the leaves withered.

The parable of the fig tree, being interpreted, is this: —

The fruit represents the love in our hearts. The leaves are the miracles or the active works. As leaves follow the fruit, so the works follow love. The works are permanent only in so far as love preceded them; otherwise they are cursed and will wither away.

So a prayer which is offered without love may sometimes bear leaves — or results — of a kind; but if the fruit of love has not first been there it is already cursed. For just as the murder-thought, symbolized by Cain, carried the curse of God on it, so the prayer without love bears the curse of Christ. Even before such a prayer is uttered it is already dead and had much better never have been born.

Another characteristic of the successful golf-player is that he puts joy into his game. Dr. Richard Clarke Cabot tells us, in *What Men Live By*, that there are three kinds of labor. One is toil that is tedious and tiresome without any hope of reward; this is drudgery. Another is activity that is unpleasant and tedious but carries with it the hope of reward; this is work. Then there is the kind of activity that is so enjoyable that one is eager to do it regardless of the reward or compensations; this is play. Every one of us can choose which of the three we will make of our own life-work. If we make it drudgery, we are slaves; if we make it work, we are men; if we make it play, we are gods. All great geniuses have made their work play. "I never worked a day in my life," said Edison; "it was all play."

Prayer as we too frequently use it is not a walking in green pastures and beside still waters; we do not throw ourselves into it with joy. We have rather squeezed it out as a lame duty, largely disliked because lamentably misunderstood, while the attitude of prayer is usually that of fear and dread, as we rarely turn to it save in direst need or terrifying disaster.

Compare this attitude of prayer with the manner in which we play. Watch the business man put away his troubles, sling his golf bag over his shoulder, and with a thrill of joyous abandon step out with a springy tread over the open spaces of the links. Contrast this with the way the same man would pray. Yet what his time in the joyous open spaces is to his physical well-being, prayer is to his spiritual health; there should be about it just as much joy.

The more joy one can put into one's prayer — joy that is built on unselfish, God-conscious thought and not an ephemeral thing of self — the more quickly will come the answer or manifestation of the prayer. For joy binds man to God, and gives him at-one-ment. It is by joy, born of the certainty of the greatest realities, that man is forever united to all that is good, and forever regenerated, apart from all that is bad. So often is the immediate sense of joy the accompaniment of the answer to prayer, that it is difficult to tell whether that sense is the cause or the sign of the fulfillment. One might better say that it is both, and yet neither: that joy synchronizes with the answer, that it is, so to speak, the brother and partner of the fulfillment, the inner realization that we are in the presence of God.

A great basket-ball player told me once that just as the ball left his hand he could tell by the thrill of joy that came to him whether or not the ball would go through the basket. In the same way many ball-players know when their bat meets the ball whether it will be a safe hit or not. Golf-players, too, by the joyous thrill which goes through them at the moment of the club's contact with the ball, know when they have made a perfect stroke. In every case the feeling of joy begins before the ball is struck and extends for some time after. May it not be that this feeling of joy takes its rise from an inner realization, a subconscious sensation of perfect mind- and muscle-coördination, which makes the perfect stroke the inevitable sequel? In the same way, when a blaze of joy comes to the one who prays it is a sign that the spiritual coördination has been accomplished — of unity with God in the first place, and unity with man, through love, in the second place — that makes the answer to prayer inevitable.

It is after one has attained this spiritual joy a few times in prayer, and has experienced the answer that accompanies it, that he truly knows that God *does* answer prayer. Thenceforth he turns to prayer with that exhilarating joy with which the golf-player turns to his game, with which Edison turns to his inventions, and with which Shakespeare turned to his play-writing. He becomes, like Paul, a genius in prayer.

As the highest peaks catch the first glow of the on-coming dawn, so a man in exalted prayer, with eyes on God, praying on the mountain top with joy in his heart, will be the first to catch the glow of the on-coming answer to the needs of man.

When you bow in prayer, then, you should not be too deadly in your solemnity; you should rather make it a joyous and exalted outpouring of the heart and mind to God. Open all the doors of the heart wide to the in-coming flood of joy; take all that you can, knowing that in so doing you are putting yourself in harmony with Jesus' own purpose in coming to man: that we might have joy, and that our joy may be full.

Know this: *that God is Love and He is also Joy.* The nearest thing to love we find in this world is joy. To get all you can of God in your heart, get all you can of joy and radiate it — joyously.

The reader may have noticed that the first three rules in this discussion of prayer, given in the form of "don'ts," are merely the opposites of the next three, which are the same rules restated in their positive form as "do's." To summarize briefly what has gone before, we may say that to pray one must simply let out Self and let in God; let out Anger and let in Love; let out Fear and let in Joy. Moreover, the reader may also have noticed that these rules, stated positively, are nothing more or less than the three jewels of Paul's rosary, Faith, Hope, and Love, restrung together in a slightly different sequence and under a slightly different terminology.

Now we come to the last part of the golfer's stroke, the "follow through." How hard it is to impress upon the beginner the value of the seemingly useless part of the golf-club swing: the letting it swing back and up across the shoulder, parallel to where it began! How hard it is to impress upon him the fact that the very power, elasticity, and impact of the stroke depend partly upon what follows after the ball has been struck!

It is the same with prayer. After a man has prayed and the answer has come, the tendency is to lean back with satisfaction, thinking that the task is completed. If this were indeed a task it might be so; but true prayer is never a task; it is a rich and blessed sharing with God. True prayer begins with God and therefore must be returned to God. This constitutes the "follow through" in prayer.

And how can prayer be returned to God? Through the gratitude that glorifies God. This gratitude is what puts the seal of permanence upon any act of prayer.

If gratitude is such an important part of prayer, then what are the avenues for expressing it? The ways and means of expressing our gratitude to God are almost as innumerable as the ways and means of manifesting love. The most direct and obvious way is to express it to God direct. Or it may be expressed to the person who was the channel for conveying God's blessing to us. Or we may return gratitude to God by passing on similar help to another. Jesus said: "Inasmuch as ye have done it unto one of the least of these my brethren, ye have done it unto me." Let us hope that some of the lepers who failed to return thanks to Christ found means of doing friendly human service to others who were in need.

We are told in Harold Begbie's *More Twice-Born Men* that when a man has been saved from sin the surest way to make his salvation permanent is for him to go straightway and save another man. And I might say that whenever we get an answer to prayer the best way to make it permanent and to ensure future answers is to go and express our thanks to God by helping others to find the same blessing that we have found.

"Gratitude, I find, is the strangest and most cleansing and strengthening feeling there is," so writes a friend. Indeed, nothing was more truly said. For gratitude cleanses out the feelings of Self, of Anger and of Fear; it strengthens the Faith, Love, and Joy that are in one. Gratitude sums up, includes, and expresses every attribute essential for prayer. Perfect gratitude *is* perfect prayer. And to keep one's self in a condition of eternal gratitude is to keep one's self in a condition of eternal prayer. Then one knows what it means to "pray without ceasing." "O Lord, open thou my lips; and my mouth shall show forth thy praise."

"Blessed be God the Father. Unto Him be the glory through all generations, for ever and ever."

When one has learned all the various parts of the perfect golf-stroke, the final task is to coördinate them in a unified and perfect whole. Perfect prayer also requires a fusing of all the various elements into one simple, direct communion.

This makes it necessary that we summarize at this point the factors that have gone before.

> *Where there is God, there is Love.*
> *Where there is Love, there is Joy.*
> *Where there is Joy, there is Power.*
> *Where there is Power, God is glorified.*
> *Where God is glorified, there is Love.*

The rhythmic round repeats itself. This is the only example of *real* perpetual motion ever known to the experience of man. It is perpetual because it begins and ends in God.

GOD

GRATITUDE   LOVE

GLORY   JOY

POWER

A straight line has a beginning and an ending. Convert it into a circle and it has no beginning and no ending.

It is from everlasting to everlasting. It is infinite, eternal.

In sports we learn the value of the circle over the

straight line. The stroke in golf begins with the club over the player's head, describes a perfect arc and follows through to complete the perfect circle. No "chop" stroke can equal the follow-through stroke in athletics, no matter whether the game be golf, baseball or tennis. Moreover, it is an acknowledged fact that the more love a man has for the sport and the more joy he puts into the stroke, the greater the force of the blow. Indeed, we may actually say that the great golfer swings his club downward with love and joy, strikes the ball with power, and follows through with the glorious and majestic sweep of the unconscious artist as his eye follows the ball on its triumphant course. The only conscious part of the stroke is raising the club for the start, and guiding it downward in love and joy. The actual stroke that sends the ball and the follow-through are the unconscious aftermath of the downward stroke.

Consider the length of the sweep of the complete golf-stroke with the fraction of an inch of space in which the club is in actual contact with the ball, and you get a pretty clear idea of the relative amount of attention you should give in your prayer to the actual *thing* you are praying for. Just as the novice in golf thinks he must put his club behind the ball and shove it along the ground, so the novice in things spiritual lays his prayer hard against his need and shoves it along. How feeble and how futile are such prayers! "But seek ye first the kingdom of God and his righteousness; and all these things shall be added unto you."

Let us carry this analogy into prayer. Start the prayer by lifting our eyes to God and stretching our mind to take in His glory. Start the prayer in Love, and Love will inspire in us Joy; then let us not think of the resultant Power that will manifest itself in response to our prayer, nor of the glory and majesty of the follow-through; rather let us *know* that these will follow — will follow as inevitably as night follows day in that vast circle in which the earth turns each twenty-four hours; let us know this so absolutely that we shall rest assured in perfect trust, knowing that he will be kept in perfect peace whose mind is stayed on God.

Every prayer thus uttered becomes an eternal prayer. Though we finish the prayer in five minutes and go away and leave it, so to speak, the prayer goes on forever, because it is a circle; because it is perpetual motion; because it came from God and goes to God; because it has no beginning and no ending. That prayer is eternal. It will continue to work for mankind until the end of the ages. The person prayed for will continue to receive its benefit as long as he lives.

It will abide with him throughout all eternity.

How can we apply this prayer to the things of the mind?

What is genius in writing, speaking, planning, organizing and creating? According to Stevenson, genius is an artist's true joy in his work. What causes one to have joy in his work? His love for that work. What is love but God made manifest in man? For the man who desires to do inspired, artistic, creative work, whether it be in writing, in business, in teaching, in speaking, — no matter what his vocation or profession, — the process of preparation is the same. He should first look to God, from whence cometh his help, then realize clearly that God expresses himself through man in Love; that Love — if it be unselfish — inevitably finds in its realization the most radiant Joy; that this Joy, founded on Love, releases infinite Power; and that this Power, released through Joy and Love, inevitably redounds to the Glory of God.

How can we apply this prayer to things of the body?

What is the source of the power of the athlete? All trainers agree that it resides primarily not in the muscles but in the condition. What is the secret of good condition? A good heart. And what is the reality of which the heart is a symbol? Love. So when praying for strength in athletics or for health in those who are sick, the process is the same — one should pray again in the perfect circle which carries

one's thought from everlasting to everlasting, begin-
ning and ending with God. Here one can realize that
the reality back of the heart is spiritual, the expression of God as Love; that this Love is perfect, whole,
pure, omnipotent; that the reality behind the blood
is spiritual — joy circulating throughout the consciousness. This Joy is pure, perfect, life-giving;
nothing can possibly prevent the perfect circulation
of this Joy, for Love is the power which circulates
this Joy throughout the consciousness; and Love is
omnipotent, for Love is God.

And what about the "follow-through?" Take no
thought for the winning of the race, the getting of
perfect health, the making of a perfect stroke. Be
not anxious for your (physical) life, what ye shall
eat, or what ye shall drink; nor yet for your body,
what ye shall put on. Is not the (spiritual) life more
than meat; and the (spiritual) body more than raiment? Keep the mind stayed on God, and know
simply that "Thine, O Lord, is the greatness, and
the power, and the glory, and the victory and the
majesty."

Those who have experienced in their hearts the
reality of the Kingdom of Heaven within know that
it is compounded largely of Love and Joy. Perhaps
the most accurate definition of heaven is: Love expressed through Joy. Remember that definition then,
when you end the Lord's prayer next time, and you

will find you have the complete circle of prayer in one sentence: —

For Thine is the Kingdom
(*That is, Love and Joy*)
And the Power and the Glory
Forever
Amen

Finally, remember the "forever." Remember that this prayer is eternal. It will stand up in the last day and plead for you. It will walk beside you at the noonday. It will be a light to guide your steps when the darkness comes. Fill the world then with such prayers, living and eternal prayers, knowing that no word of God will come back to you void, but that bread cast upon the waters shall be found again after many days.

Praying on the Mountain

THERE is a beautiful symbolism among primitive peoples, extant in the times of the prophets of Israel and extending clear down to Jesus' day, that the abode of the Most High was in the mountain. "Who shall ascend into the hill of the Lord? or who shall stand in his holy place?" "He that dwelleth in the secret place of the Most High shall abide under the shadow of the Almighty."

Moses, we know, went up on Mount Sinai to commune with God, and we read that Jesus went frequently into the mountain apart to pray. But we do not have to go to Mount Sinai, "neither in this mountain," according to Jesus; for whoever prays retires — symbolically — into God's holy Mountain. Have we not often in our prayer said in our heart, "I will lift up my eyes unto the hills, from whence cometh my help," and where is there any more beautiful expression of trust than this: "O send out thy light and thy truth . . . let them bring me unto thy holy hill, and to thy tabernacles."

The Mountain is symbolical of praying with the uplifted thought, that is to say, with the mind fixed on God. The higher the thought — the higher we ascend into the mountain — the further we are removed from the petty ills and troubles in this world and the closer we are to God and Heaven. As we start to climb the mountain of prayer the world-thoughts still cling close around us and we find that we are kept pretty busy protecting ourselves from their claims. But as we rise higher, where the vision is broader and the air is clearer, the petty troubles and annoyances of this world dwindle in the distance until, if we continue far enough, we reach the place where protection against them is no longer needed. When we finally reach the summit we discover that all we have to do is to keep our thought on God and His goodness, and realize that heaven with all its harmony is round about us here and now, and our troubles vanish before us like mists before the sun. This is getting "up into the high mountain." And Isaiah tells us how the whole world will "beat their swords into plowshares, and their spears into pruning-hooks; nation shall not lift up sword against nation, neither shall they learn war any more," when the praying in our churches becomes of this exalted nature, that is to say, when "the mountain of the Lord's House shall be established in the top of the mountains, and shall be exalted above the hills; and all nations shall flow unto it."

The references in the Bible to the "top of the mountain" are allegorical references to the highest type of prayer that it is possible to conceive. They describe the condition of prayer that Jesus attained. He stood at the very summit of prayer, and everything on earth was made subject to him. Jesus had no need of the denial in life, because to Him there was nothing to deny. He stood at a vantage point where He could look straight through the symbolism of facts to the Truth beyond, and by means of His correlating, harmonizing synthesis of vision, expressed through parables and miracles, bring all things into harmony.

Since the first chapter in this book I have hardly once used the terms "denial" and "affirmation." Why? Simply because you and I have been climbing a mountain: we have been very rapidly outgrowing them, leaving them behind. When they have reappeared at times they have usually appeared in somewhat different guise and under other terms. The imagination, for instance, has taken over the office of the affirmation and proved far more effective and adequate to the situation. Up to the present we have spoken of nothing which can stand forth and take over the office of denial.

And what, after all, is the function of denial? Is it not our weapon of defense, our shield and buckler, just as affirmation is the sword of attack? The knights of chivalry discovered that the more expert they became in attack the less use they had for the defense. Is not this also the philosophy of our modern knights of the gridiron, the arena, and the tennis courts, — in football, boxing, polo, basket ball, and tennis, — that the best defense is an irresistible attack? And when an attack becomes absolutely invincible, something which nothing can stand before, there automatically ceases to be any need for defense at all. This explains why Jesus never used the denial excepting in two very serious cases, where he was raising people from the dead; and in both those cases he used it to drive away the thoughts of limitation—not from his own consciousness, but from the consciousness of those who were about Him; and in each case the denial took the form of a creative parable: "The maid is not dead, but sleepeth." This utterance was like the chivalric act of a knight of old, who knowing himself to be impervious to the arrows of the enemies, nevertheless did not scorn to lean forward and interpose his own glorious shield, to ward off the attacking arrows from the bodies of weaker brethren. In other words, while Jesus stood on the summit of the peak, He did not forget that there were in the great throng many who were still lingering near the foot of the mountain.

May we too hope to reach the mountain top where our prayers may become a simple and direct reaching out for the good, instead of a puttering and fretting over things that are bad? Will our attack ever become so irresistible that we too may use the sword only, and throw away the shield and buckler?

It depends upon how utterly we give ourselves in trust to God, and how completely we open our imagination as a window for the light of God to shine through us. It depends upon how successfully this inner light can reveal to us that the earth which appears to be flat is actually round; that the man who appears to be bad is actually good; that the tapestry of God's infinite plan for us is not a patchwork of hideous designs but a magic web of marvelous workmanship and infinite beauty. For the imagination, when illumined by the light of God, — as explained in a former chapter, — shows us unities, harmonies, and beauties where the unimaginative mind sees only separations, discords, and ugliness. But with most of us poor humans, who give our imagination only partly and not wholly to God, we find that after it has converted nearly everything into harmonies and unities there still remain scattered bits of discord, of separation, of ugliness, which, like chips that fall from the woodcarver's table, cannot be correlated and unified into the universal scheme of things.

What shall we do with these chips that fall by the way? Deny them? If you will be patient with me I will show you a better way.

When God blessed us with the imagination to see the harmonies and congruities and logical relationships in this world, He blessed us at the same time with the sense of humor, to see the inharmonies, the incongruities, and the illogical relationships in life and laugh at them. Moreover, humor enables us to see these things without malice and without fear; it transforms them, rather, into the means of giving us diversion, rest, and enjoyment, so that they actually enrich our store of human experience, become assets and not liabilities in the possession of our heart. A teacher can eradicate a pupil's fault by laughing at it more quickly than by any punishment. Doctors can cure people of trivial complaints by laughing them away better than by surgery or drugs.

So we may say that the laugh is the spirit which denies, just as the imagination is the spirit which affirms. Both are needed for a sane, practical, and substantial spiritual life. The one is useful to protect us against relativity, the other is needed to carry us forward into infinity. One represents the Falstaff of our nature, the other the Ariel; one the Sancho Panza, the other the Don Quixote. But the further we climb up the mountain in our quest for the perfect prayer, the less and less we have to depend upon the Falstaff and the more and more we can depend upon the Ariel to fulfill all our needs. As John the Baptist — he who came to make the way straight by denying the bad in man — said when he saw the Son of Man approaching, the one who was to affirm the good in man: "He must increase, but I must decrease."

I made reference to two occasions where Jesus interposed His denial like a shield to protect those about Him who were weaker than Himself. Let me give an example of where He used His sense of humor to protect and save others who were near Him. The Pharisees took great pride in their ability to understand spiritual things. And in spite of their manifest faults it is true that there was a great deal of real piety among them. However, there was one colossal evil in their midst that, for some reason or other, they could not as a class easily escape; this was their bondage to hypocrisy. In order to help them to see the ridiculousness of this bondage Jesus painted a series of word pictures that for sparkling humor and brilliant sarcasm have no equal in literature. In one of these pictures, for instance, he described a learned and sober scholar carefully straining out a gnat from his soup and then proceeding to swallow a camel with its immense hump, long, hairy legs, and long, scraggly neck. Merely to visualize this picture would be enough to set an Oriental audience into roars of laughter. If these words had come from the mouth of Sancho Panza or Falstaff, students of literature would be saying to this day that there had been nothing funnier in all literature. That Jesus' heroic treatment of this serious situation in the hearts of the Pharisees brought forth fruit in later years, converting many of the younger Pharisees to join his followers, is evidenced from the mention made in the Book of Acts of the very influential place held in the Apostolic Church by men who had formerly been Pharisees.

By humor and laughter of course I do not refer to the low, coarse type of buffoonery. I mean the exalted, spiritual, joyous type of laughter. Laughter that is compounded of love and joy and gratitude is divine laughter, whose echoes are heard in heaven. It is such laughter that sends us tripping higher and higher up the mountain. The more evil that comes upon us and the more we find ourselves able to laugh at it lovingly and joyously, the quicker we shall reach the stage where no evil can touch us; for as the touch of Midas converted everything into gold, so can the touch of heaven-born laughter convert every shadow and bit of darkness into golden bits of sunshine to brighten and gladden our path.

When Hercules wrestled with Antæus he found that every time he threw him down upon the ground the enemy arose stronger than before. But when he discovered that Gæa — the Earth — was the mother of the giant, and that every time her son fell back upon her bosom he rose with renewed strength, then Hercules changed his tactics. Lifting Antæus high in the air, away from the source of strength, he held him there till he brought him into subjection.

We, who are not children of Earth but children of God, could learn much from the lesson of Antæus. We too, whenever troubles cast us back upon the bosom of our Father, rise with renewed strength. But just as Antæus let Hercules, who was smaller in stature than he, lift him away from the source of his power, so circumstances, infinitely small and trivial, may drag us away from God. Troubles, misfortunes, disappointments, and handicaps, if they but throw us back upon God, if they merely give us opportunity of bringing into play our God-directed imagination and our heaven-blessed sense of humor, may become converted into marvelous good fortune. For trouble, if it merely turns us to God and hence renews our strength, ceases to be evil, and becomes good; it becomes the best thing that could possibly come to us, next to God Himself. For our growth in power and happiness depends upon the number of seconds out of each twenty-four hours that we are resting in God.

Had Hercules continued to throw Antæus back upon Mother Earth often enough, the giant would have risen at last so strong that neither Hercules nor any other creature could throw him down. Thenceforth the giant would no longer have required any weapons of defense, for he would have possessed within himself all the strength of his mother; he would have become invulnerable, invincible, irresistible, for he and the Earth-strength would have become one. And so it is with us. After trouble has thrown us back upon God a number of times, our strength will become so great that thenceforth trouble no longer can toss us anywhere, for we shall abide in our Father, and His strength will abide in us. This use of trouble Jesus had in mind when He said: "Blessed are they that mourn. . . . Blessed are they which are persecuted. . . . Blessed are ye when men shall revile you . . . and say all manner of evil against you falsely for my sake. Rejoice, and be exceeding glad: for great is your reward in heaven." And what is this reward in heaven if it is not this at-one-ness, this unity with the Father? As Antæus might have achieved dominion over all the physical creation had he ever attained sufficient unity with his Earth Mother, so may we hope to achieve dominion over our little world of time and space, if we can only attain sufficient unity with our Father.

And now, because we are near the summit of the mountain, let us pause and take one look back over the path we have trod, filled as it is with cast-off weapons of defense and attack, outgrown garments, axioms that no longer serve us, rules that no longer rule, commandments that no longer command. For, like Dante when he passed from the leadership of

Vergil to the leadership of Beatrice, we too have come out from the reign of law and have come under the reign of grace. And as we pause and consider what has happened within us, this great realization comes to us: *Axioms, laws, commandments are not the Truth until they have been incorporated into a life and have life.* The one condition of Truth, according to Jesus, is that it be *alive*. Any axiom, law, or commandment which is not used is dead. This is as certain as that seven times one is seven. Jesus declared, "Blessed are they that hear the word of God *and keep it*." This is one implication in all of Jesus' teachings which is not sufficiently understood. It accounts, among other things, for His frequent reference to His own life, His own personality, as though He considered it greater than His teaching. It was greater! He did not say, "Follow my teachings," He said, "Follow *me*." He did not say, "My teachings are the way," but "*I am* the way." He did not say, "My teachings are alive," but "*I am* the life." He did not say, "My teachings are the truth," but "*I am* the truth."

Perhaps one reason for our common mistake in thinking that Truth is something that can be confined in books is due to our dictionary-makers who treat Truth as a noun — something static — when it really has the positive, dynamic quality of a verb. This is peculiarly true of Truth as Jesus used it.

For Jesus never dealt with people, facts, or formulæ from the outside, but always from the inside — that is to say, from the point of view of the Spirit. This accounts for the fact that whenever He discussed Truth He spoke not as the scribes, who clothed it with vestments of laws, dogmas, and outward things, but "as one having authority," because He spoke with that freedom with which only those who live and move and have their being on the unconditioned basis of Spirit can speak. In other words, when Jesus used the word "Truth" He always meant *the Spirit of Truth*. And the Spirit, as we all know, cannot be brought into captivity to any form, any formula, any concept. When a man thinks he can confine the mighty rhythms of God within the narrow confines of law and logic, and believes he can measure the very frontiers of Infinity with fragile and feeble theories, hypotheses, and formulæ, he is deluding himself even as Thor deluded himself when he believed he could drain the cup whose contents were linked up with all the seven seas.

The Spirit of Truth, like the Spirit of Love, or the Spirit of Joy, is a condition of Consciousness or a state of Being. It is the Spirit which brings us into at-one-ness with All-Truth. It is a state of perfect discernment, perfect understanding, because of perfect unity with the Father. Truth, then, as Jesus used it, is not a concept. *Truth is the power to conceive*

and to express concepts. It is an eternally active principle, ever operative, ever available, ever eman-
cipating man. It is not dead, but lives — the Living
Christ in man. "I am the truth," said Jesus. "Ye
shall know the truth and the truth shall make you
free." For Truth, as Jesus used it, is not statistics;
it is not statements, — even the aphorisms of the
wise, — it is not laws. For statistics will grow old,
statements will cease to be applicable, laws will fail;
but the power to conceive and express Truth will
never die. This power is eternal; it comes from God
and it goes to God; it is the one thing which continually lifts man God-ward. It is the Holy Ghost
working in man.

This, then, is what awaits us at the top of the
mountain — this unity with the Spirit of Truth.
To attain this, everything else is but a means to an
end, and when it has served its purpose we may, if
we wish, cast it aside as we would an outgrown gar-
ment. That is why I say: when you have outgrown
Denial and Affirmation, you may throw them away
without any regret. You may even abandon Humor
as a necessary means of growth in spiritual life, if
you find yourself able to bring everything into
harmony, unity, and beauty without it. And how
can we tell whether to-morrow or the next day we
shall not find something even greater than the Imagination for opening doors to the love of God — for

finding our absolute and unconditioned oneness with the Father?

For this reason man will continually reach new concepts, use them, and pass on to find others. One concept of Truth after another will come and go. But the power to conceive and express concepts, the power to realize and live Truth, will remain eternally in the heart of man. This is the power that links man to God, that brings him into harmony with the Divine. This power is what Jesus referred to when He said, "The kingdom of God is within you." And so, while not all of us agree upon the exact meaning of every teaching of Jesus, while we may not be able to comprehend all the Truth of every statement He made, we are all able to comprehend that He had the power to conceive and express Truth, eternally, universally, instantly — that, in short, *He was the Truth.* And only in so far as we also conceive and express Truth shall we understand His promise: "Ye shall know the truth, and the truth shall make you free."

This, then, awaits us at the top of the mountain — this freedom that comes from knowing the Truth. Then we shall know what the Scripture meant when it said of man, "As he thinketh in his heart, so is he." All that we shall need to do will be to look at the thing, the need, the problem, the trouble, with Faith, Love, Joy, and Gratitude — in other words, with our hearts and minds stayed on God — until we can see through the thing or fact to the Truth or Reality which abides in it or is behind it. Once get this inner realization clear enough and the thing or fact will fade into its native nothingness and the Reality within will take its place. The inharmonies will fall into harmonies, the ugliness will turn into beauty, and the dissociated parts will reassemble in marvelous unities.

Nor will this require effort on our part other than merely to be conscious of the Living Presence of God in us. Just as the rain needs only to become conscious of the sun's rays shining in it for the rainbow to become manifest in the heavens, so we shall need only to become conscious of God shining in our hearts for the fulfillment of prayer to become manifest upon earth. Just as the action of the sky upon the earth can bring marvelous harmony, symmetry, and beauty into being, so the action of God upon man can also bring into being marvelous harmony and symmetry and beauty. Moreover, the result in both cases follows naturally, automatically, and inevitably. No effort, no striving in either case is required, merely a letting go and *letting the light shine in and through*, and the rainbow of fulfillment will appear in the sky.

The rainbow is one of the first great symbols mentioned in the Old Testament, the symbol of answered prayer. It appeared to Noah, but he would never have seen it with his physical eyes in the sky unless he had first seen or "thought it in his heart." For it was merely the reflection or refraction of what had already taken place in his own heart. Had he not first prayed a perfect prayer in his heart, he would never have seen the perfect manifestation in the sky.

I referred in the preceding chapter to the perfect prayer — the prayer that has no beginning and no ending, because it begins with God and ends with God; because it is a circle. The rainbow is an outward symbol of such perfect inner communion. The rainbow as seen by man, limited and circumscribed as he is by the bounds of earth, is only a half circle; but the rainbow as seen by God is always the perfect and complete circle. The rainbow as a spiritual symbol is never seen save from the point of view of Heaven. Noah with his mortal eyes could see only half of the promise of God; the rest he must needs see with spiritual eyes. The ordinary man sees only the phenomenon of nature or the half circle; Noah saw the promise of God because he saw the completed circle. But again I reiterate: he would not have seen God draw a perfect circle in the sky had he not first seen God draw a perfect circle in his own heart. For again we must remember that as a man thinketh — and prayeth — in his heart, so is he.

Helps to Prayer

How, then, can we pray the perfect prayer in our own hearts? How can we become conscious of the rainbow within, in order that we may be a witness to the rainbow without? By attaining to a consciousness of absolute Love, absolute Joy, absolute Gratitude, and above all of absolute Oneness with the Father. Once attain this consciousness and everything we think, say, or do comes from the Father. Once attain this condition of mind and Facts turn into Realities, the sick become whole, the lost become found, and sinners become redeemed. And how can we attain that consciousness of Faith, Joy, Love, and Gratitude? By thinking of God, or our highest conception of God; of Heaven, or our highest conception of Heaven. Some can look straight at God direct; some can look through a beautiful sunset into the Kingdom; some can look through the face of a friend straight into the face of the Father. Some can sit down and convert the situation into a parable; others can turn it into a psalm. Every church has its form, its ritual, its individual method of appeal, to bring the mind and heart of its devotees into a condition of consciousness conducive to finding God.

Our chief problem is how to keep the mind stayed on God and keep the eye single, that is to say, filled with the illumination of Love and Faith and Joy, and keep out the darkness of anger and fear and selfishness. To steady the mind and hearts of the people and to keep their eyes filled with light, the psalmists of old composed prayer-psalms. Because many have sought such comfort in these modern days, and often sought in vain, I have added to this chapter a few simple prayer-psalms, which I hope may steady some mind and keep some eye filled with light.

A Psalm of Faith

OUR Father, Thou art infinite, eternal, omnipotent, and omniscient.

Whether I take the wings of the morning, behold, Thou art there.

Though I make my bed in Sheol, behold, Thou art there.

Though I go to the furthermost parts of the sea, Thou art before me.

Thy Love is as infinite as the sky is infinite, and Thy Spirit as pure as the morning dew.

Thy Power reaches as far as the east is from the west, and Thy Wisdom is greater than all hidden treasures.

Thy Peace is closer than the atmosphere that wraps us round, and Thy Joy is brighter than the sun at noonday.

Thou art continuously shedding down upon us Thy Wisdom, Thy Joy, and Thy infinite Love.

Make us as pure as the morning, and as powerful to serve Thee as the winds that blow.

We would be branches of Thy living Vine,
Fountains of Thy living Water,
Windows for seeing Thy Truth,
Channels for bringing Thy love to men.

We of ourselves are nothing, but with Thee we are all things.
Open wide for us the doors and windows of our soul.

Direct our steps and guide our ways,
For we are Thine — wholly, utterly Thine,
Closer to Thee than breathing,
Nearer than hands and feet.

We would be filled — filled with Thee, O Father,
That we may give — give — give to the uttermost,
That Thy glory may be made manifest in man!

A Psalm of Love

Thou and Thy Love are infinite;
Thy Love therefore fills all space,
There is no space where Thy Love is not,
Otherwise it would not be infinite.
It is filling the very space which we are occupying,
Here and Now.

That Love is in us and we are in that Love.
We could not escape it if we would,
And we would not if we could.
It abides in us and we in it.
Therefore when we let go doubt, and irritation, and self,
And resign ourselves completely to the great All-Power
That resides within and about us,
We *are* Love, even as God is Love.

God then speaks through us,
Thinks through us, acts through us;
For when we speak, we speak Love,
When we think, we think Love,
When we create, we create Love;
For God always does his work by means of Love
    made manifest in man.

A Psalm of Joy

We know, O Father, that perfect Love expresses itself in
    perfect Joy.
This Joy radiates throughout the vistas of consciousness
As sunlight plays up and down the vistas of mountains.
No power can possibly prevent the perfect circulation of
    this Joy,
For it is propelled by Love,
And Love is omnipotent;
For Love is God.

This Joy is pure, perfect, complete, and life-giving,
And it is continuously revealing itself in infinite Power
    and infinite Glory,
Expressing the eternal Majesty.
This Joy is absolutely pure, untouched by anything unlike
    Thee,
Therefore this Joy is perfect, whole, and complete,
Bringing wholeness, healing, and perfection.

    Nothing is sick but this Joy can make whole,
    Nothing is impure but this Joy can make pure,
    Nothing is hid but this Joy can bring to light,
    Nothing is imperfect but this Joy can make perfect.

For this Joy is omnipotent Power,
Made manifest in man,
Irresistible, infinite, eternal,
Circulating with unfailing regularity and ease
Throughout the vistas of consciousness.
Nothing can possibly prevent the perfect circulation of
    this Joy,
For it is propelled by Love, and Love is omnipotent; for
    Love is God.

A Psalm of Inspiration

We know that Love is perfect understanding,
For Love is the light which makes all things clear,
For Love is the giving up of self to the Larger Self,
So that the Larger Self pours through us as through a
    channel,
And this activity of Love is perfect Wisdom, is perfect
    Understanding,
Bringing perfect Inspiration, perfect Peace, perfect Joy.
When the Larger Self speaks, all knowledge, past, present,
    and to come,
Speaks through us without check and without limit,
For that which is in part is passed away,
And that which is perfect has come.
For man, standing rooted in eternal Love, relaxed to its
    eternal harmonies,
Makes of himself a conch
Through which the music of the spheres finds voice and
    utterance,
And man, divested of self and expressing Thee,
Stands witness to Thine imperishable Glory.

A Psalm of Wholeness

Bread cast upon the waters
   Shall be found after many days;
As we measure
   So is it meted unto us.
He who gives all
   Receives all in return;
He who gives wholeness
   Receives wholeness in return;
And he who gives himself wholly
   Shall himself be made whole.

Our Father, help us to give ourselves — not as the world
   giveth, but *wholly* unto Thee.
Without qualification or exception or condition or com-
   promise we give ourselves unto Thee.
Complete, finished, and whole is the giving;
Absolute and utter is the surrender.
Thy rod and Thy staff alone shall support us;
Thy yoke and Thy burden alone shall we carry.
Take us — not in part, but complete and whole,
For in Thee alone shall we find all Completeness and all
   Wholeness,
And man, the child of Thy Love and the heir of Thy Glory,
Reflects and expresses this Wholeness and Completeness.

This complete outpouring of self gives us perfect Peace,
   infinite Peace.
Nothing can prevent our finding this infinite Peace,
For it abides all about us, in us, and through us;
Before ever the world began it was there,
And through all eternity it shall be there;
The perfect Peace that comes from perfect surrender to Thee.

For Thou art the Lord of Peace,
Our abiding place in all generations,
Our Rock and our Fortress.
Whom shall we fear?

O God, giver of every good and perfect gift, Who giveth
perfect Peace,
There is no place where Thy Peace is not, for it is infinite,
And we, when we put ourselves completely at rest in Thee,
Eternally abide in this Peace, the Peace of Mind that
passeth all understanding.

A Psalm of Harmony

We lift up our eyes unto the hills
From whence cometh our help.
Though the reflection in the water may quiver and ruffle
And conceal Thy great beauty at the beck of the winds
and tides,
We know that Thy Truth shall never quiver or shake.
Though discord and misunderstanding may appear in the
world below,
We know that if we lift our eyes unto the hills
We shall see the Reality is clear and beautiful and eter-
nally harmonious.
We know that the more the reflection vibrates in wind
and tide,
The more stable and calm stand the everlasting hills.
The more the opposite sides of the mountain appear in
the reflection to be pulling all things asunder,
The more permanently above they are seen holding the
mountain in place;
And the further the tip of the reflection sinks down into
the depths,

The higher the glorious dome pushes its peak into the heights above.

Give us grace, O God, to see the world of Reality right side up and not upside down.

May we see the mountain — not the reflection in the pool.

May we see behind every argument the Truth that draws it into Love;

Behind every angry thought, the Love that vibrates it into eternal Harmony.

We pray, O God, that we may look up, lift our eyes, and see Thee as Thou art,

And see Man as Thy child, made in Thy perfect and eternal image and likeness, as he really is,

       Eternally reflecting Thy Harmony,

       Filled with Thy Holy Spirit,

       And abiding eternally in Thy Love.

A Psalm of Abundance

The infinite ideas of God continually come to man:

Ideas of Beauty, Service, Leisure, Power, Abundance, Harmony, and Happiness.

Man receives these ideas in perfect symmetry and sequence,

And rejoices to pass them on to give joy to his fellow men,

Receiving beautiful, perfect, and infinite ideas in exchange,

According to the perfect rhythm of God's infinite Love.

God has always placed man in the right place

For the receiving and passing on of these perfect ideas,

For man is led and governed by God,

Who governs the stars in their courses

With perfect rhythm, and with perfect regularity, and with perfect ease.

There never was a need that did not have its own supply
    residing within it,
Nor was there ever a question that did not have its own
    answer concealed within it,
Nor ever a yearning for Hope or Love but carried its own
    fulfillment.
Who would put a seed in the ground and then plant a
    stalk in the ground above the seed?
For the stalk grows out of the seed — from within it, never
    from without;
So the answer grows out of the question, the fulfillment
    out of the need, and the Love out of the yearning.

So ask, with Love, and it shall be answered;
Seek, with Love, and it shall be found;
Knock, with Love, and it shall be opened;
For as air, soil, and water are to the seed,
So is Love to the question, need, and yearning.
For without Love all prayer is as sounding brass or a
    tinkling cymbal
            That profiteth nothing.
            But Love never faileth.
            Love casteth out all fear,
            Love is perfect understanding.
            Love is its own realization,
            Its own completion,
            Its own fulfillment.

A Psalm of Guidance

We know, O Father, that man is not responsible for making
    plans,
For Thou art the only Designer.
We know that no one ever *makes* plans;

For plans grow as flowers and trees grow,

Are things of life with roots, ramifications, and inter-weavings,

As beautiful as tapestries, as permanent as the eternal stars.

May our eye be always single, our vision always clear as light,

That the radiance of Thy infinite Love may light our path forever;

That we may see Thy plan as it eternally is,

In all its beauty, in all its harmony, in all its grandeur,

And see ourselves as we always are —

Thy children, made in Thy image and likeness,

The perfect expression of Thy perfect direction,

Each instant conscious of Thy perfect ideas in perfect succession.

As Thou keepest the stars in their courses,

So wilt Thou guide our steps in perfect harmony, without clash or discord of any kind,

If we but keep our trust in Thee.

We know Thou wilt keep him in perfect peace whose mind is stayed on Thee,

Because he trusteth in Thee.

We know that if we but acknowledge Thee in all our ways

Thou wilt direct our paths.

For Thou art the God of Love,

Giver of every good and perfect gift,

And there is none beside Thee.

Thou art omnipotent, omniscient, omnipresent,

In all, through all, and over all,

> The only God.

A Psalm of Gratitude

Our Father, we worked for Thee till we thought we should
  become weak in Thy service,
But Thou hast renewed our strength; we have mounted up
  with wings as eagles.
We gave unto Thee our all,
But Thou hast filled our barns with grain.
We gave ourselves utterly to Thee, without stint and with-
  out measure,
Only to find ourselves returning to meet ourselves, clad in
  garments of glory.

> We made ourselves completely captive to Thy will,
> And behold, Thou hast set us eternally free;
> We let Thee have complete dominion over us;
> And behold, Thou hast given us dominion
>   over every living creature.

How can we ever thank Thee, how can we ever repay Thee,
  Thou Lord of our lives?
For even the thanks we send forth to Thee upon the wings
  of the morning
Return bearing gifts in the evening.
All we can do is to continue to give — give — give to the
  uttermost.
All that we have is Thine; all that we are is Thine.
Take us, use us, we cannot be exhausted;
The more we are used the more beautiful, the more eternal
  we become.
Thou hast set a Well within our hearts that springs up
  unto eternal Life.
Thou hast set a Light within our hearts that radiates
  eternal Love.

The Soul's Sincere Desire

And the light of Love shining through the fountain of Life
  reveals the rainbow of Joy,
Joy that is eternal, unending, complete,
The perfect promise of Thy perfect fulfillment.

Accept our thanksgiving, our praise, our gratitude
without stint and without measure,
O Father,
For Thine is the Kingdom and the Power and the Glory
forever and ever.
Amen